Treasure of the Mind

Treasure of the Mind

A Tale of Redemption

J. Michaels

RESOURCE *Publications* • Eugene, Oregon

TREASURE OF THE MIND
A Tale of Redemption

Copyright © 2009 J. Michaels. All rights reserved. Except for brief quotations in critical publications or reviews, no part of this book may be reproduced in any manner without prior written permission from the publisher. Write: Permissions, Wipf and Stock Publishers, 199 W. 8th Ave., Suite 3, Eugene, OR 97401.

Resource Publications
A Division of Wipf and Stock Publishers
199 W. 8th Ave., Suite 3
Eugene, OR 97401
www.wipfandstock.com

ISBN 13: 978-1-60608-963-7

Manufactured in the U.S.A.

To my son Christopher
May he live forever

Contents

Preface ix

Amazing Grace 1

Michael's Pain 3

Damn Those Dreams 5

Poker with the Boys 7

Moving On 9

Finding Wayne 11

Wayne's Secret 15

Carlsbad by the Sea 18

Solomon 22

Restless in Carlsbad 25

Emerging From Darkness 28

The Battle 31

Freedom is Just a Word 34

Be Careful What You Ask For 37

Journey into Hell 40

Digesting Pelicans 42

Naked at the Window 47

Wisdom by the Sea 51

The Sink Hole 54

Re-living the Past 57

Forgiveness 101 61

Practice Makes Perfect 64

Just Another Day at the Beach 68

Hot Java 71

The Whale 76

A Day Off 81

The Last Lesson 84

Saying Goodbye 90

Leaving Paradise 93

Homecoming 95

A New Beginning 99

Preface

MY SON'S UNTIMELY AND premature death at the tender age of seventeen left me in despair. Christopher was the youngest, the most troubled, and in some ways, the most precious of our children. He was the only kid I knew (and we raised six) who could go directly from being lectured, berated, and grounded, to the shower; where he would then proceed to sing uninhibitedly, as if he had not a care in the world. He was creative, loving, and had a great sense of humor. He was also a lousy juvenile delinquent. My wife and I love the story of the time he was chased on foot by the mall police. He wore, as was very popular at the time, the baggy jeans that so vividly allowed his boxer shorts to show above his belt, which by the way, did not serve him well in his escape attempt. Although we did not see it firsthand, the hilarious image of him running from the police and stopping every few feet to hike up his jeans was just too much to bear. After he somehow managed to elude his pursuers, he stopped at a nearby store for a soft drink, where he was then promptly taken into custody by those same people who had, by now, caught up to him.

After I learned the most important thing about having a son, I stopped spending all my time trying to fix him and spent more time loving and appreciating him. On one of our visits to the juvenile detention center where Chris was spending some time, I remember telling him that he should give up his attempts at crime not because it was wrong, but simply because he was so bad at it. It was possibly the first time in a long time he actually listened to me regarding his problems.

Chris was a great kid; he had a huge heart, a great disposition, and enormous potential. But Chris lost his biological mother when he was just five years old and he never fully recovered from that greatest of all rejections. Although my wife did her best and was a great influence on Chris, his wounds were too deep for any stepmother to heal. His pain could only be relieved by attention of a greater magnitude than any offered by anyone else or, as it turned out, by the exaggerated interest of rebellion. Chris never stole for himself; he stole for the attention of those who offered him what he so dearly needed. He stole to replace the maternal love lost. I remember the first time he was caught stealing shortly after his mother left. He took a pocket knife from a friend of the family, took it to school, and promptly gave it away. Despite our best efforts, this pattern would continue intermittently into his teenage years, where it would be fueled by the insecurity and awkwardness of that troubling phase of life. In his search for his troubled and hiding soul, my son gave his allegiance to the wrong person. That person, whom Chris once considered to be his best friend, took his life.

For several months after his death, I struggled with grief, guilt, and anger. And then I learned how to forgive. I attribute that learning to a book called *A Course in Miracles*. I also attribute my eventual redemption to the same tome. For some time after my son's funeral and the ensuing trial and conviction of his killer, I felt a need to tell the story of how I survived this greatest of all tragedies; that of losing a child. This book was born of that need. But like so much of life, stories are a blend of fact and fiction. I like to call it *faction*. This book is *not* an entirely factual account. It is instead, the story that emerged from my soul in the form that it was meant to be created in. Like Chris' life, it is a tale told not only with pain and grief, but more importantly, with joy, humor, and hope. It is a story I cherish as a tribute to my lost son. I will leave you to ponder what is fact and what is fiction. I have truly exercised my poetic license, but in the process, a story worth the telling, and I believe the reading, has been born.

Amazing Grace

Her solitary voice filled the silence of the funeral parlor. The words of the song pierced my heart, driven deep into my soul like a dagger thrust. The song I loved so much, now a dirge for my lost son.

> *Amazing grace, how sweet the sound*
> *that saved a wretch like me!*
> *I once was lost, but now am found,*
> *was blind, but now I see.*

I was blind. I never really knew my only son and now he's gone.

> *Twas grace that taught my heart to fear,*
> *and grace my fears relieved;*
> *How precious did that grace appear,*
> *the hour I first believed!*

I was graced by his life and wasn't smart enough to see it.

> *Through many dangers, toils and snares,*
> *I have already come;*
> *Tis grace has brought me safe thus far,*
> *and grace will lead me home.*

Oh God, I don't know if I can survive this.

> *The Lord has promised good to me,*
> *his word my hope secures;*
> *He will my shield and portion be,*
> *as long as life endures.*

My only son, what have I lost?

> *Yes, when this flesh and heart shall fail,*
> *and mortal life shall cease;*
> *I shall possess, within the veil,*
> *a life of joy and peace.*

Amazing Grace

I hope Chris has some peace now. Will I ever?

> *The earth shall soon dissolve like snow,*
> *the sun forbear to shine;*
> *But God, who called me here below,*
> *will be forever mine.*

I can't stand this. I want to die.

Michael's Pain

Nothing I can do will make this go away. I didn't know pain like this was possible. Why is it when you need the days to go by quickly they go the slowest? I screwed up as a father and I know it but I don't deserve to lose my only son, a son I hardly even knew. Well, I guess that part was my doing. I just couldn't see past his problems. All I could think about was how to fix him, how to make him into a good person. Hell, he was probably always a better man than me, even at seventeen. They don't tell you about the regret, it's the worst part; all the lost ballgames together, the growing up that I wasn't there for, the passages, and the eventual man-to-man talks. And now it will never happen.

It's just not the same with girls. I love my daughters dearly but a father and a son bond is something only a man can understand. A son touches a different part of you than a daughter. There are things that can only be shared by two men. I wanted so much to see the day when we talked about his life and I helped him through it. I wanted to be his best friend. I wanted to be his best man.

I need to move on, right? But move on to what? Everything feels shallow now; no depth, no satisfaction, and so far from happiness that even death looks better. What if nothing ever feels good again? I guess I can always drink or drug myself into oblivion. What if that doesn't do it? I'm scared, I can't live like this.

Michael's Pain

Emptiness prevails
Darkness has chased away the light
My soul aches for redemption
To go beyond the pain
Agony so deep it pierces my soul
Don't hate me, my son
Though failed I have
To see you truly and pure
Lend me some time, my Father
Let me go back
To treasure what once was put off
And know its sweet moment again

Damn Those Dreams

I love Bob Dylan. Gracie can't stand him but I think he's a genius. His words are always popping into my head and there's just something about that raspy voice that I really relate to. Bobby and I have grown up together and he's the poet I always wished I could be. "I don't give a damn about your dreams" he says in his latest, greatest classic. I love it as usual but damn Bob, this was one dream I cared a lot about, just a gunshot and a funeral too late.

My mind rambles a lot these days, from one pointless thought to another. I need something that turns my crank again. I need for one of those pointless thoughts to mean something again. I have the big office, a six-figure income, an impressive home, and a new beemer. And none of it means anything to me. The girls and Grace have been great and I truly love them. But even they can't lift this heaviness that hangs over me, weighs me down, and maybe some day soon will devour me.

I guess it's time to call Jimmy and see if he still grows that great weed. I need something to keep me from going where it hurts so much. Maybe a poker game with the boys will help. We can drink beer, maybe smoke some pot, and get crazy. I love those guys but I don't know if I'll be able to stomach their inevitable pity. No reason to pity me, I'm the one who blew it with Chris. I'm the one who passed by his childhood like he would be waiting for me when I finally decided to be there for him. Dreams be damned. They don't wait for us while we waste our time chasing the buck, and the career, and the toys that we value so much.

Maybe I should consider going back to work. But then I'd have to deal with all the well-meaning sympathy that does nothing for me except remind me of what I'm trying to forget. At least I could get lost in the endless details, the useless meetings that will hush when I walk in. The problem is I just don't care about all that anymore. I wish I could leave my skin and deaden my feelings. Maybe a new dream to replace the one I messed up or just something else to be more pissed off about than I am about the kid who killed my son.

Damn Those Dreams

Regret gnaws at me
Eats away my being
Let me escape this torture
Let me not be
Why must I choose
Between despair and hate
Shall I kill to save me
Will it salvage my soul
Will it tame the beast
Or destroy my hope
I know not where to turn
I have lost sight of love
Erase my mind and feelings
Ease my suffering heart
Lord, come save me
Before I fall apart

Poker with the Boys

Here I am pounding beers and playing poker with some of the best guys in the world and even that is empty. And damn, they're afraid of me. I can see it in their eyes. They're afraid of where I've been and of where I am, afraid to get too close to it.

"Guys, we need to ratchet this party up a notch. Let's crank up the music and get this shindig going. How about some *Eagles* or *Dire Straits*?" I call out, hoping to drown out the thoughts. Nervous laughter that just doesn't fit these guys forces its way out. But they're trying. They're my friends and they want me to feel better.

Jimmy breaks open the baggie and loads the pipe. "Tom, turn up the music and give this man some rock and roll," he yells across the room. "And let's get the pizza going before the damn munchies set in."

"Mike old buddy, what's your pleasure, *Dylan* or the *Eagles*? Jimmy's got all the good ones. He's more of a *Dylan* and *Eagles* freak than you are," Tom calls out as he rifles through Jimmy's CD collection.

"*Hotel California* and crank it up, way up. If I going to lose all my hard-earned money to you jokers, at least you can serenade me while you're doing it." Real laughter comes this time. For just a minute, we all forgot.

"Who needs a beer?" Mark offers as he beelines to the fridge. "Let's get this party going." But the nervousness starts to seep back in . . .

Not a bad night, things could have gone worse. At least I didn't lose it in front of the guys. With all the booze and pot we consumed, a lot could have gone wrong. Who would think a bunch of sports-loving, foul-mouthed, middle-aged guys could be so sensitive and selfless? It's good to have friends, even if they can only distract you for a couple of hours on a Saturday night. Maybe I'm drunk and stoned enough that I'll sleep tonight, maybe.

Poker with the Boys

*My brothers confirm me
Clumsily offering hope
Agreeing to be distracted
From insidious plague inside
Attempting to defer my temptation
To slit my hated throat
Offering a sliver to live for
Friends to fill the void
If only for a moment's persuasion
Hoping to help me hang on
Offering drink and herb
Soothing with words and music
To keep me diverted
From despair's lonely door*

Moving On

Man, this rush hour traffic never lets up. The windows are down and the music is popping but I'm nervous as hell about facing all those people at work. I better get over, my exit's coming up. Damn, I missed it. I guess I'll just keep going. Let's check the console. If I remember right, Jimmy handed me a joint after the poker game. Where did I put it? Here it is, a big fat ugly one! You would think that a guy that's been smoking pot as long as Jimmy has would have learned to roll a good joint by now. What the hell am I doing? Its 8:15 on a Monday morning and I'm cruising past work and lighting up a joint; me, mister reliable, mister taking care of business. So what, it's only a job and they'll cut me some slack. After all, my son just died and I've lost a lot more than an occupation. No work today, time get away.

It's better now. The weed has my mind soothed and the wind in my face sure feels good. You know, right now I don't really care what happens. I could even drive right into a tree and except for the possibility of coming out crippled instead of dead, the thought of it doesn't even scare me. Like Janis Joplin said, "Freedom is just another word for nothing left to lose." Hey, pull yourself out of this morbid crap. You've got a lot to live for; a great home, a loving wife and family, and a high-paying job. You're just short one son, your only son.

I need to do something before I turn into an addict or a drunk or a pile of maimed flesh on the side of the road. Who can understand this kind of loss; loss of a son and loss of a life that used to mean something to me? The guys are great but most of them have the same kind of life I do and it still matters to them. Who do I know that just doesn't care about it, someone who knows something I don't about getting some meaning out of life? Wait a minute, what about my old buddy Wayne? He taught me meditation and he got me through that rough patch with Gracie a few years back. He always seemed so peaceful and content with his life, even with that old pickup and dinky little apartment. We lost track of each other when I got to be such a big shot at work and thought I was too good to hang out with him. And, oh yeah, he had a teenage daughter who hung herself a few years ago. I need to talk to Wayne; he'll know what to do!

Moving On

Fading, comfortless, and alone
Wrapped in a meaningless life
Providing no warmth or shelter
Driving down lonely highway
Only the herb for company
People in my dour life
Mean nothing any more
Dare I flirt with death
One quick flick of the wheel
And pain is gone
The grim reaper my newfound friend
Hope's light shines in faint glow
Insisting I remain for a better day
Perhaps an old friend can lend me
Comfort and reason to stay

Finding Wayne

Last time Wayne and I got together was at this great little vegetarian place where his girlfriend worked as a waitress. Vicky was closing in on forty but she still had a great body and a smile that warmed you all over. In fact, the first time they met was one night when Wayne and I came in for one of our coffee talks. We used to visit different places just to try their coffee and to see if they had a good place where we could solve the world's problems. That particular night, we had walked into the Gemini restaurant, looked around, and found our own table in a secluded corner booth. Then Vicky walked over, flashed that killer smile of hers, and asked us what we would like. Wayne looked up at her and I might as well have been invisible for all the attention I got after that. I might have been pissed if I hadn't been married but Wayne was such a great guy and it was a real joy to see two people connect like that. Anyway, they hit it off immediately and the Gemini became our hangout after that, at least until I got too successful to hang out with an ex-hippie who drove a pickup. What a jerk I must have been. Here was this great guy who had a crystal clear mind, a huge heart, and a boundless spirit and I couldn't see it or appreciate it. A lot like how I treated Chris, I guess; how ironic.

Last I heard, Wayne was working near downtown Denver at a place called People House; some kind of new age place or counseling center, I think. He would make a fine teacher or even a therapist. He seemed to always know more than everyone else, even us degreed university bigots. I wonder if they're in the phone book. It must have been at least three years since I last saw him. The way I treated him, I'd be lucky if he would even talk to me.

The following week I figured what the hell, what do I have to lose? So instead of heading home after work I decided to make a stop at the Gemini and see if Wayne or Vicki, or anyone who knew them, was still there. I hadn't been around for awhile but maybe someone there would remember our numerous coffee talks. I walked through those same hand-carved heavy oak doors, a little more weather-beaten now but they still gave the place an air of naturalness and character. I stood there for a minute just soaking it all in, remembering all those great times we had; all the late-night talks, the coffee, the great food, the warm glow of the place, and the friendly people who worked there, all came rushing back to me.

"Sir, can I help you? Sir? Are you here for dinner?"

My attention snapped back to the present. "Uh . . . not really. I'm looking for someone, an old friend." I turned and looked into the eyes of a stunning young girl, the kind restaurants always put upfront as hostesses. But like most of the people I remember who worked at the Gemini, she too seemed to have an air of calmness and ease that you only see from people and places that are comfortable with themselves.

"Sir, would you like to look around for your friend?"

"Sure," I replied in a sort of half-aware response. Not like me to be so removed from the moment, but this was different. It was different because sitting in the corner looking directly at me was my old buddy Wayne. After all this time there he was in the same place where we had talked about so many different things years before. "I think I just found him," I said, as the hostess smiled and walked away.

"How long has it been, my friend?" I said, as I approached the table. I hoped he still considered me a friend but I really didn't know what to expect. He looked at me for a minute without saying a word. Then a smile, that wonderful, honest, accepting smile, emerged. He stood up, still without saying a word, and walked over and put his arms around me. I returned the hug and it was as if no time had passed at all. It felt just like those warm, healing times that I had taken for granted so long ago. In that instant, I remembered what it was like to be loved unconditionally by another human being. There was no withholding, no reservation, just an old friend welcoming me back.

"You've lost some weight," he finally spoke.

"Well *you* look as good as ever. Doesn't time ever affect you? Other than being slightly greyer, you would never know you aged at all." I found myself gushing like a teenager and I was surprised by the joy I felt at seeing this very special man again.

"So how are Grace and the girls?" It was odd that he didn't include Chris. He knew him so well and they were pretty close at one time. Of course, Wayne always had a way with kids. They gravitated to him and he always seemed to be surrounded by children who he somehow managed to enthrall with the simplest of things. One minute he would be talking to you and the next he would be off leading a bunch of them on a rock hunt or a bird-scouting adventure.

"Grace and the girls are doing fine. You know Grace; she always seems to keep all of us on an even keel."

"You don't look like a person on an even keel, my old friend." Wayne was never one to waste time with a lot of small talk. He was only ever interested in talking about things that really mattered to him and he had a way of making them matter to you. "In fact, you look like hell." I felt the tears coming. In the presence of this gentle man whom I hadn't seen in years, I was about to cry. What the hell was wrong with me? I had controlled the feelings so well up to now, being strong and putting on a good show for everyone.

"You still don't mince words, do you?" After a long pause and from somewhere deep inside me, I added, "I *am* in hell."

"I know," he said simply and with great kindness. We both just stood there. I was frozen in this sudden surge of grief and Wayne waited for me. "Sit down, brother," he finally said. "We'll have some coffee and talk, just like old times." With those oddly comforting words, we both sat. "Tell me about your hell and we'll see if there's a way out." So we ordered coffee and we talked.

"Gentlemen, I'm sorry but we are closing and as much as I hate kicking you both out, my husband would like to see me before he goes to work in the morning." Those words broke the spell, a spell that had lasted for nearly six hours. At that precise moment, I realized that I had, for however brief a time, felt whole again.

"Well old buddy, this is my treat in more ways than one," I said as I handed the waitress a twenty and told her to keep the change. As we walked together to the parking lot we were both silent, as if savoring something very profound. "I'll call you," was all I said as Wayne got into that same old beat-up, blue pickup truck. He just smiled and nodded as if he knew that I would.

Finding Wayne

Oh sweet joy, light in my darkness
A warm heart welcomes me back
Distracted from anguish for a moment
Not so alone now
The hope light shining brighter
Basking in the past with beloved friend
Sheltered so slightly
From present's steely dagger
My Father's presence offered
Through old blue truck diplomat
Finally presenting simple love
Adversary to hate and desolation
Soothing my soul in parity
With hope lost and forgotten

Wayne's Secret

I NEVER CALLED WAYNE again. I didn't need to. A few days after our last meeting, without any prior arrangement, I simply walked back into the Gemini and there he was again, at the same table, watching me walk in as if he fully expected me to be there at precisely that point in time. "You're a little late but that's okay. I just asked Carla to bring us some fresh coffee. Sit down my friend and let's help you find your way home." Wayne is such a complex but yet simple man, right to the heart of the matter before the first cup of coffee had been delivered.

So again we talked. Our first meeting had been all about what I was feeling and where my head was at; an outpouring of controlled grief, followed by an attempted synthesis of feelings and thoughts. How I felt and what I thought about how I felt seemed to be what was prompted to emerge. But now we talked about healing. Wayne had helped me through a rough patch a few years ago and the same words he used then that helped so much again surfaced in conversation.

"Lean into the pain, Michael. You know what lies on the other side of it. It's the same. It's just a lot more pain this time." At that moment, I suddenly realized how afraid of that pain I truly was. He was right of course, but I didn't know if I could survive this one, even with his help.

"I don't know buddy. I don't know if I can do it. I may die in the process."

"You know, I might agree with that except for one thing. The one thing is that, as you and I both know, there is no death. I know it consciously and you know it in your heart. The problem is that your heart is shut down right now and you're afraid to go there."

I had no idea what the hell he was talking about but I trusted him and his wisdom. "Tell me what I should do dear friend. I'm lost and all I can see is shadows," I uttered in a weak and defeated tone.

"I can't help you," he said simply. In that moment, I lost what hope I had managed to summon and I wanted to fade into oblivion. Our time together had given me a glimmer of optimism and the promise of some sliver of happiness returning to my dark and battered soul. "I can't help you. But I know someone who can," I heard from the dark abyss I had so quickly started to sink back into. Those last few words brought me back and I looked at Wayne and he was smiling again; that same caring, knowing, impish grin.

"Don't ever do that to me again or I will kick your old, grey-haired ass," I responded. We both laughed out loud in a mixture of pain, hope, and friendship. We laughed so loud that everyone seated near us stopped what they were doing and smiled along. Damn, it felt good. It had been so long since I really felt like laughing.

"I know a very special man. You may not know this, but I'm not a carpenter anymore. I'm a therapist. I do individual counseling and I run a men's group on Tuesday nights. I still teach meditation which, by the way, you could probably use."

"So, if that's the case, why are you recommending me to someone else?" I said, even more confused by the sharp turn of events.

"Because he can help you and what you need is beyond my skills," he replied. "This man is responsible for changing my life and he inspired me to become a therapist."

My first thought was *oh yeah, another therapist with his walls filled with diplomas and certifications, declaring to the world how wise and caring he is*. "But you're the best therapist I know and I didn't even know you were one," I countered. Wayne paused, and then looked up at me with compassion like I have rarely seen one human being have for another.

"My dear friend and brother, I care about you enough to *not* be your therapist. I care about you enough that I could never live with myself if I tried and failed. Solomon will not fail you. I trust him even more than you trust me. If you give him a chance, he will help you recover your lost soul. He *will* show you the way home."

I was still dazed by Wayne's unwillingness to come to my aid. Our talks had given me hope again and now he was blowing me off. But I did trust him and I knew that he was truly a good man. If it had been anyone else I would have ignored him and went my own way, no matter how doomed it was. "I'll try it," I finally replied. Wayne smiled, a look of relief and completion taking over his face. "So where's this super therapist located?" I asked half-heartedly.

"California, sunny southern California," he replied. "Do you like the ocean?" he added.

"We'll see," I said.

Wayne's Secret

Pain is the devil's handmaiden
A weapon to impale upon
Fear, its lowly sidekick
Misdirecting to games of aversion
To avoid the immutable destruction
Yet love hides nothing
And tolerates no secrets
Refusing to leave pain unattended
Nor avoids fear's deceptions
Love sends angels to attend us
If we but yield and pray
There to bring us home again
No matter how hazardous the way
Listen well to fair angel
And follow where he leads
From depths of despair and suffering
Pay attention to Heaven's plea

Carlsbad by the Sea

I HAD NEVER BEEN to Carlsbad. In fact, the only Carlsbad I had ever heard of was in New Mexico. As the United Airbus skimmed over the top of downtown skyscrapers and touched down on the runway in gorgeous San Diego, I couldn't help thinking about what kind of man could have had such an impact on a person I considered to be wise beyond his years and circumstance. I guess I would soon find out.

Carlsbad, as it turns out, is a beautiful coastal village right on historic Highway 101, about thirty miles north of San Diego. As I exited Interstate 5 and steered towards the ocean, the peace and beauty of the place somehow soothed my troubled mind and made me feel oddly at home. I was starting to understand why Wayne spoke so affectionately about this place. But if it was as special as it appeared, why had he come back to Colorado?

As I turned onto the 101, I was almost overwhelmed by the brilliant sun, the cool ocean breezes, the breaking waves, and all the happy people walking around. Outside of the usual crowd events, I had never seen so many people outside before and they all seemed to be very pleased with where they were. This place was already starting to pierce that heart armor Wayne had accused me of having and I had a vague sense of the possibility of healing.

The Carlsbad Inn is an older hotel located about a block from the ocean. It lacks the business feel of a *Marriott* or the touristy trappings of the stereotypical *Sea Breeze* type of lodging. It holds the same charm as the town itself, unpretentious in a way unlike how most people think of southern California. Wayne had recommended the Inn and it fit him, a quality place with grace and style but not conscious of it; a relaxed, easy-going lodge that fit perfectly into its surreal like environment. I parked the rental car in front of the hotel right across the street from a quaint little coffee shop and removed my lone suitcase from the trunk. I didn't plan on staying long but I felt I owed it to Wayne to see what this Solomon guy was all about. Little did I know what I was about to get myself into.

After unpacking and getting settled in my room, I decided to take a walk along the beach. It was a weekday in September so the beach wouldn't be as crowded and I needed to clear my mind of all the thoughts that had been racing through it for the past few days. Carlsbad has a pedestrian seawall that runs parallel to the beach and so I started my walk there. As I passed people going in the opposite direction, I was surprised by the number of people who smiled and openly greeted me. This place and these people definitely did not fit the stereotype of the southern Californians I had been warned about. One older guy in particular made an impression as he passed. The openness of his smile reminded me of Wayne's and I could have sworn that he spoke my name as part of his passing greeting to me. I looked back at him only to see him doing the same. Oh well, maybe I was becoming attractive to other men. Grace always said she thought I had *gay* in me. I call it balance but denial runs deep, so who knows?

After walking on the seawall and sitting on the beach for a couple of hours, I headed back to the Inn. In that short time span, I had seen pelicans performing vertical dives for food, surfers carving waves, and a multitude of other sensory impressions, some in very small bikinis. I was relaxed but suddenly very tired. Maybe a short nap would help. It had been a long time since I slept for more than an hour or two at a time. The last thing I remember before dozing off was a cool breeze wafting over me and the clock clicking over to 3:33pm.

The sun streaming through my window woke me and the bedside clock informed me that I had slept almost fourteen hours! I had slept more in the last day than I had during the previous week combined. I was beginning to like this place more all the time. On the other hand, it could have been a simple case of fatigue and exhaustion overcoming and shutting me down. Either way, it sure felt good to feel rested again. For the first time in awhile I actually wanted to get out of bed. I seemed to remember a little coffee shop nearby and I could sure use some caffeine to clear up my sleep hangover. After an uncharacteristically extended shower (I was usually a get in and get out kind of guy), I threw on some shorts, a t-shirt, and my recently purchased, beach-standard flip-flops.

The coffee shop was already filling up and it was just past 7am. It was truly *another beautiful day in paradise,* an aphorism I had already heard twice since arriving. The hand painted sign above the open door read *Café*

Elyssa and as I walked in, the smell of freshly baked pastries and coffee filled the air. One small table in the corner set opposite a counter and display case for the pastries. Outside, bordering the sidewalk and facing the ocean, was another five or six tables and two fire pits with seating for another five or six at each. I thought about grabbing a seat at one of the communal fire pits but hesitated, knowing I wasn't ready to socialize with strangers no matter how friendly they were. Instead, I paid for my coffee and decided to take a small table with two chairs back in the corner. I arrived there at exactly the same time as an older white haired gentleman only to realize that it was the same guy I saw on the seawall yesterday! I offered the table to him and he responded by gesturing for me to sit also. My first instinct was to politely decline and just take my coffee and go but there was something about this guy that intrigued me.

As I set my coffee down and pulled out my chair, he said, "How are you Michael? It's nice to finally meet you."

Carlsbad by the Sea

*Heaven's aid comes in varied forms
A book, a dream, a vision
But the hand of God comes mainly extended
Attached to arms of friends
Blessings wrapped in familiar terms
Or as strange as alien fruit
Synchronicity with unknown agenda
Delivers in simple terms
All that is needed or prayed for
Unexpected and often missed
Where I seek its wisdom
In clarity amid ocean's mists*

Solomon

"Do I know you?" was about all I could think to say. How could this man, whom I had never laid eyes on before yesterday, possibly know who I was? With the exception of the exchange of pleasantries on the seawall, we had no previous contact. This was getting strange but something told me to go with it.

"At some level, yes we do know each other," he replied after a pause that seemed extraordinarily protracted. He seemed to sense my uneasiness and then added, "We met yesterday down by the beach. Don't you remember?"

I nodded and took a sip of my coffee, hoping to buy some time. Here I was in a beautifully strange new place having coffee with a guy who felt oddly familiar but whom I knew I had never met. And he knew my name! "How do you know my name sir?" I finally got up the nerve to ask.

"Wayne told me," he said, in that same simple style that instantly reminded me of Wayne.

"Are you Solomon?" I somehow managed to blurt out, still dazed by the implausibility of the situation.

"I am," was his answer.

"We had an appointment to meet tomorrow at your office."

"I know, but don't you think this is so much better?"

Although he answered my questions, this strange man seemed as illusive as one of those passing ocean breezes. Not in an evasive way but somehow seeming to cut through the non-essentials and getting down to what mattered.

"Are you suggesting I spill my guts to you in the middle of the coffee crowd?" I said, becoming a little irritated.

He looked into my eyes for an uncomfortably long time before responding, "I'm suggesting we talk." His gaze left me feeling naked, like he already knew everything there was to know about me. My instinct was to write the whole trip off, pack my bag, and get the hell out of there. But that same mind whisper that got me here calmed me and I decided to stay. "I've been told that before," he said, out of the blue.

"Been told what?" I managed to say.

"That I'm a strange old guy."

How the hell did he know that? Had I thought it out loud? Could he read my mind? "Damn," was all I could manage in response.

"Why don't you sleep on it tonight and we'll meet here again tomorrow?"

"Okay," I said, as another feeble reply fell from my lips. Pretty damn poor response coming from a business executive who regularly presented to large groups of people. Here I was dumbfounded by one little old white haired man. I stood, looked at him for a minute, sat my coffee down, and just walked away.

Solomon

The mind is a mysterious place
A labyrinth of cryptic avenues
Unknown even to its landlord
Roamed well by Creator's enterprise
Those with mind so expansive
Gain access to boundless realms
Able to see quite clearly
That which eludes those of lesser sight
Born in time and space
To aid us in recovering the light
Fragile babe or little old man
Illumination the prize

Restless in Carlsbad

I WALKED AROUND TOWN for the better part of the day but I couldn't tell you much of what I saw. The place felt magical but it was a blur to me as I kept returning to my thoughts about this strange little man and how he seemed to know me in a way I didn't understand. He had uttered only a few words but it was enough to disorient me and put my mind in a place that was profoundly uncomfortable. Over and over, I considered packing my bags and getting out of town. The words from one of my favorite songs by the *Eagles, Hotel California* "*. . . you can check out but you can never leave*" flashed in my mind. It seemed so strange and quite frankly, sent chills down my spine.

After hours of walking around in a semi-stupor, I checked my watch only to discover that it was almost dinner time. I found myself in front of a magnificent Victorian style house that just happened to be a restaurant and they had a bar. And I needed a drink, at least. The bartender was a young blond guy in his twenties probably trying to make enough money to keep his days open for surfing. He flashed a pearly white smile and greeted me with the same casualness that was so prevalent here.

"I'll take a Rob Roy," I said, "and keep them coming." After several of my favorite alcoholic concoction, it was evident to me that the events of the day and the booze had taken its toll. I let my young bartender friend talk me into some food and they delivered it right to the bar. I woofed it down the way you do when the booze or pot munchies strike; fast and furious with a minimum of chewing involved.

After the blitz of booze and food ended, I tipped my newfound surfer/bartender buddy and headed back to the hotel. Luckily, there was only one main street to cross or I might not have made it back. The disorientation of the morning had only been exasperated by the day-long wandering and alcohol consumption. So after nearly getting run over and bumping into a couple of very tolerant locals, I managed to get to my room. The room was just getting dark enough to lull me into a half-sleep and eventually, blessed oblivion.

Sleep was no more forgiving than being awake. Dreams of dark places and distorted images filled my mind. I was looking for something very important but had no idea what it was or where to look. Was it my soul? Was it my son? Was it my death? I was overwhelmed by the fear of the possibility of never finding what I so desperately sought. I wandered for what seemed like an endless time and distance in a fluid spongy world that had no firmness or foundation. As my desperation neared the breaking point, I heard a soft, gender-less voice say "*There is nothing to fear, your brother waits.*" The peace of the voice brought the same tranquility to me and for a time, I was truly serene. I thought I might survive.

Restless in Carlsbad

Strange wanderings in paradise
Fueled by confusion and fear
Looking to numb impending pain
Trying to forget the unforgettable
Hoping to forgive self-inflicted guilt
Seeking help and fearing it
A little old man assigned me
I can't stand to open the gate
To let him try his hand at healing
All that remorse and hate
Sleep, blessed sleep
Let me think no more
Forgive my reticence
To open that door

Emerging from Darkness

I awoke with the confidence that I had a chance; a faint possibility of something happening that was better than my life had been for these past few months. What that *something* was still eluded me, but at least there was some hope left in me. This trip had been truly strange but somehow I knew it was not pointless. Still tired and confused, I got out of bed, showered, dressed, and headed for the coffee shop. Straight espresso was definitely the order of the day.

Things were looking up. Even though the outdoor area was almost full, there was no line and I went directly to the counter. The same petite, dark haired woman with a French accent, who waited on me yesterday, took my order. No smile from this one, but at this point the espresso was enough. I ordered a double shot cappuccino and an onion bagel. I needed some serious fuel for this day. I had no idea what it held for me but whatever it was, I knew it would be different. Feeling unusually optimistic, I took my order and paid with a ten. As I turned to leave without my change, my raven haired mademoiselle allowed a tiny smile and we shared a brief moment. As I turned back around to look for a place to sit, I noticed only one available chair. Solomon once again smiled and motioned for me to join him.

"Good morning, my new friend. You look barely better than the last time we met. Did you sleep well?"

"Well sir, I toured the town, got drunk, and finished it off with a not so sound sleep," I answered.

Then silence... Solomon just looked at me. In fact, he looked directly into, no not into, but directly *past* my eyes. It was as if he would not be denied access to my mind, but not in an sinister way. But rather a way that felt oddly comforting, accepting, and even loving. I barely knew this strange old man but here I was after a short greeting, letting him inside me. After what seemed like several minutes, he smiled, took a drink of his coffee, and looked away towards the ocean. "Another beautiful day in paradise," he uttered as if it were expected.

"Yes it is," was all I could muster. Once again, I found myself speechless.

"Shall we start our work together?" he said after a few minutes more of silence.

"And exactly what would that work be?" I replied.

"The work of saving your soul, of course," he responded with a directness that caught me by surprise.

Again I found myself speechless, surprised by this man but somehow believing that he just might be able to do what he proposed. I was used to authority coming from a job title, money, physicality, or a badge. But this serene, confident, little white haired man exuded an authority that came from none of these but was stronger and more certain than any power I had ever encountered. I simply replied, "Okay." I was becoming a man of few words, a trait never before attributed to me. "Yes, let's do exactly that," I added. He looked directly at me, smiled, and bowed his head ever so slightly.

"It will be my honor," he replied, almost in a whisper. After a few more moments of silence, Solomon opened his eyes from what seemed like a prayer and said, "My office is bounded by the ocean, the sun, and the sky. Our sessions will start here with coffee and end with a morning walk along the beach, if you agree. Perhaps even the dolphins will join us. I can't think of a better setting, can you?"

"No Solomon, I can't. When do we start?" I asked.

"Tomorrow morning, after a good night's sleep, my friend." I stood, extended my hand, and he took it. But he didn't shake it, he just held it for a second or two, just long enough that I felt I would weep if he didn't let go.

"I'll see you in the morning, Solomon." And I left.

Emerging from Darkness

*Sunrise always brings me hope
If but only for a moment's consideration
Hope springs eternal in light
Giving birth to optimism's flight
Now this person before me
Offering to save my soul
Dare I accept or deny him
I know not which way to go
Yet he touches me in ways unknown
Stirring ancient memories
Archived among mind's gold
Part of me hopes to live
Part of me wants to die
Dear Father, please grant me
Fair courage and the wings to fly*

The Battle

Like almost every moment that I had spent in this heavenly little town, the time after I left the coffee shop was a blur. But this time it wasn't a drunken haze, but rather a dreamlike quality that made every thing, every place, and everyone I encountered seem lighter and less dense. As I drifted past the hotel clerk and headed for my room, I kept seeing Solomon's emerald green eyes and remembering how I felt when he took my hand. These were the last thoughts I remembered the next morning after I awoke from some of the most restful sleep I had ever had. No dreams, no tossing or turning, and never conscious for a second. It was almost as if I had completely disconnected from my life here, almost like I had died. And I felt fantastic!

I cannot remember a time in my life when I wanted so much to get out of bed and get going; a feeling in stark contrast to the heavy, druggy, feeling I experienced nearly every morning since Chris died. Something had come alive in me and I couldn't wait to see my new friend and counselor. Luckily for me, there was a mirror on the wall near my room door or I would have left without my pants! People are pretty casual in southern California, but that may have been a little too informal even for them. I stood there laughing at myself for my foolishness and finally sat down to regroup.

What the hell was I doing? Here I was in a town I had never seen before, rushing to see an old man I barely knew, and doing so with an almost childish enthusiasm. Me, the buttoned down, sophisticated executive going to a therapy session in sandals and shorts to be counseled by a stranger on the beach. Every rational part of me wanted to stop this roller coaster ride, change my clothes, and get on a flight back to Colorado as soon as my un-tanned highlander legs could carry me. The elation of a few moments before drained from my body, and the all too familiar darkness of the last few months resumed its former foothold. I sat there, feeling so much less alive than I had just a few moments before. The sadness, the grief, and the depression all returned. I felt dead again. Why couldn't I just die? Maybe I would rest again like I had last night. Nothingness was preferable to this.

As I sat there trying to decide between life and death and not even having enough energy to choose which way to go, something inside me started to fight back. There was a part of me that wanted to live again, to be happy again, and to hold my wife and daughters in my arms again. Damn it, I was better than this. I would not go down without a fight. I would not let this darkness overcome me. And if this little old man could help me do that, then screw it, I was going for it. Sitting pant-less there on that hotel room chair, I fought the battle for my life. I chose to live. I would see what this strange little man had to say.

The Battle

Up and down I go
Heaven and Hell, the locales for foes
Two parts of my self adversaries
Vying for my soul's control
Hope and despair clash in battle
Pulling me here and there
Whom shall I side with
Chosen as partner to be
Who beckons the strongest
To take over the confused me
The dark of despair attracts me
So much easier to just give way
And let it take me over
And deliver me where it may
The light also beckons
Though pain stands in the way
To survive and live forever
Requires more than I can pay
My courage may abate me
And leave me stranded near hell
But if it may lend comfort
And Spirit finds me well
Brave the dark waters I shall
Til holy river takes me unrestrained
To ocean's vastness
To healing, at long last attained

Freedom is Just a Word

"Good morning, Solomon," I said as I walked directly up to him, forgetting to stop for my morning caffeine fix.

"You seem to have fared well," he replied, with the most genuine smile imaginable. Did he know about my inner turmoil of that morning? Did he sense how close I was to leaving, to giving up?

"I knew you would be here," he added, with the same confidence that permeated everything else about him. "Shall we walk?"

"Lead the way," I replied, and we headed for the seawall that bordered the beach. It was just past 7am and the seawall was starting to fill up with smiling, energetic souls out for their morning walk or ride or run. The sidewalk above the seawall resonated with the sounds of cyclists whizzing by, people greeting each other, and the grating sound of the occasional skateboarder. We exited the seawall at one of the several entrances to the beach and emerged onto warm, white sand. My feet sank in and I had an immediate urge to go barefoot, something I hadn't done since I was a kid growing up in Detroit. As I removed my sandals, I noticed that Solomon had already removed his and left them on the seawall.

"Aren't you worried someone will take your sandals if you leave them there?" I asked, feeling foolish as soon as the words left my mouth.

"Does it matter?" he replied, without looking back as he continued walking towards the surf. My petty thoughts soon dissolved into the sounds of the waves hitting the sand and the beauty of this wonderful place.

"Why do you want to die, Michael?" he finally spoke after a protracted silence.

"What the hell are you talking about?" I responded instinctively.

"You want to die. You thought about it again this morning," he replied, without the slightest hint that I had even said anything.

"What makes you think I want to die? You barely know me and you think you know something that personal about me?"

"Michael, we *all* share mind. The difference between you and I is that I know that and you are afraid to know it."

Now I was getting pissed. "Who the hell do you think you are, telling me I want to die and that I'm afraid? You don't know squat about me," I spewed.

"Your anger betrays you, Michael. If you were free of your fear, you would have nothing to defend, nothing to be angry about." Again, silence . . .

My anger subsided and suddenly despair came crashing down on me again like the waves that were hitting the shore in front of me. He was right. This little old man knew me better than I knew myself. I *was* afraid, afraid to go on living. And I was angry that I had wasted away my time with my son and now I would never get it back. We stood there in silence for what seemed like an eternity; Solomon staring at the ocean and me staring into the depths of my soul.

"*We are brothers Michael and I will help you. But you must be willing to let go of your fear and your anger. They are not your friends and the comfort they give will someday destroy you. They are not the way. But there is a way out and I will take you there if you are ready, if you are willing to learn to live.*"

Even though he never *spoke* those words to me, I knew the thoughts were coming from him. I could only stand there and look down at this wise, gentle man, and cry; in broad daylight, on the beach, with tears streaming down my face. I felt completely naked and I didn't care. My heart was crushed and I simply didn't care.

I'm not sure how much time passed before I looked over and realized that Solomon had left. I could see him in the distance walking slowly down the beach; his shirt off, his feet playing in the surf, and his snow white hair tossed by the ocean breezes. He seemed so peaceful. I felt so broken.

Freedom is Just a Word

Life turns corners at a moment's notice
Never thinking to pause or care
What threat lurks around those corners
To flatten a fragile man's faith
Riding waves of optimism
May end on reef or rock
The higher the wave
The harder the fall
No safety net or protection
To hinder what comes to call
Simple words that pierce one's heart
Unveiling emotion well hidden
Brings me to my knees it does
No leave granted to conceal
Confronting all that enrages me
Forcing me to feel
I lean through the pain
No alternatives in sight
Broken down in tears
Deciding on fight or flight

Be Careful What You Ask For

I AWOKE WITH A jolt. What time was it? How long had I slept? Crap, I missed my appointment with Solomon. Quick shower, brush my teeth, and out the door. Crossed the street, almost hit by a car, swore at the driver, and there he was. Even though I was almost an hour late, there he was, sitting in exactly the same place as the day before.

"You realize that time is completely irrelevant, don't you?" he said, obviously toying with me. "Get some coffee, my friend. You look like you need it. Or at least you look like you believe you need it. Either way, get me one too will you?"

As I brought the coffee back to our table, Solomon smiled at me and I couldn't help but ask, "I'm not even sure why I bother talking to you old man. You seem to know what's on my mind before I even say it." As soon as the words left my lips, I remembered what he had said to me the day before about *sharing mind*.

"And there you have it Mike, asked and answered," he said, as he sipped his coffee. We drank our coffee in silence. For some reason I can't fathom, silence seemed to be the right thing. We finished our java, looked at each other, nodded, stood up, and headed for the beach. I was beginning to believe the spoken word was greatly overrated.

We continued to walk in silence until our feet hit sand. Then Solomon, as if he were addressing the sky and the ocean, said "I am responsible for what I see. I choose the feelings I experience, and I decide upon the goal I would achieve. And everything that seems to happen to me, I ask for and receive as I have asked.[1]"

I was stunned. Was he telling me that I had asked to have my son die? That I wanted to go through this horrible loss of any meaning in my life?

"Do you have any idea what has happened to me, old man?" I responded, aware of the self pity in the background of my mind as I spoke.

---

1. A Course in Miracles (Foundation for Inner Peace, copyright 1996) Text - page 448.

Why was I even considering this? Because no matter how ludicrous it seemed on the surface something deep within me whispered that he was right.

"I would never wish this on my worst enemy, much less myself and my family," I said, but at the same time having a vague feeling that what I had just said wasn't completely true.

"*You* are your worst enemy, Michael. And you and your family, including Chris, agreed to this."

Now I was not only shocked but instantly furious. I wanted to put my fist right through this old codger's face. I was so mad, I was speechless. Before I could respond, Solomon looked into my eyes with the most gentle, caring look I had ever received from another human being and said "The only way to heal fear, anger, and guilt, is to forgive. You can't undo any of this but you can forgive your son's killer and, more importantly, you can forgive yourself. Learning to truly love yourself will make you whole, perhaps for the first time in your life."

Again, the anger instantly evaporated. He was right. I was angry. I was filled with fear disguised as anger and I felt guilty as hell for letting my son down. And I didn't love anyone right now, much less myself. In fact, I hated my son's murderer, myself, and God for taking Chris from me.

"Sit with your thoughts my friend and we'll talk again tomorrow." Solomon gently touched my face and then left.

Be Careful What You Ask For

Turmoil again, nothing deterred
Straight to the heart of the matter
So little regard for suffering
No pity offered as balm
Rage still slightly hidden
Available to silence my muse
If only he would abide me
Leave the sleeping dogs lie
But not to be, his acquiescence
His goal not deterred at all
No anger provoked in return
Only love to soothe the beast
How may I deem to adopt it
This gentle offering aimed to heal
Broken enough to accept it
Bid it enter and make itself real

Journey into Hell

How could I forgive this monster who had so viciously slaughtered my beautiful boy? How could I forgive myself for pissing away the short time we had together? How could I forgive my God for allowing this to happen? I could not. But I also knew that if I didn't, I would die from the inside out, eaten alive by these insidious feelings. They would consume me and I couldn't let that happen. Grace and my girls needed me and I needed them. And I needed my God back, the God I had shut out but I knew had never really left me. Solomon was my only hope and I knew it. At some level, I knew that God had sent him to me, to heal me, and bring me back from this hopelessness. This was my chance, maybe my last chance, and I would not blow it this time.

I slept for almost the entire day, and I dreamed. I dreamed of hideous demons and dark repulsive places. I dreamed of lost souls, caught up in despair and their own self-inflicted hell. And I knew I was among them. I fell into deep holes and came face to face with contorted faces filled with fear and rage. I saw sharp threatening colors that pierced my soul. I have never been so afraid in all my life, awake or asleep. After what seemed like an eternity roaming this tortuous, dreadful place, I came to the edge of a cliff. Below me, I could see nothing but the darkest black imaginable. A void with no visible bottom and a place with no light, no love. A place of despair and emptiness and it beckoned to me. All I had to do was take one more step and my suffering might be forgotten. But I also knew it would not be healed and the price would be very steep. A part of me wanted to end it at any cost but another part still held hope of redemption. As I stood on that precipice trying to decide between living and dying, I saw a faint silhouette on the other side of the chasm.

"*You can never die Michael, but you must choose to live. You are lost but not forsaken and God but waits for your decision. He will wait for eternity, but can you?*" the voice whispered across the gulf as if it were pure thought carried by the wind. "*What is your decision, my Son?*" My mind filled with the most comforting and loving warmth I had ever known, and I stepped back. I would go on.

Journey into Hell

*Dreams of Hell torture me
Its demons and screeching sounds
Pulling at something unholy
Intending to take me down
To depths unheard and dreamed of
To neighbor with suffering souls
Laying my soul to waste
Erasing memory of Home
Awaiting only my consent
To join the demon parade
Discarding love of God
The only fee to be paid
I step to the edge of the precipice
Look down at my offered fate
An abyss of loveless hate
A golden voice calls out
Asking me to reconsider
The toll of taking that step
Love offered as surrogate
My guide to a better fate*

Digesting Pelicans

When I finally awoke, I realized that I had reached a turning point, a fork in the road. I had chosen to live and I knew that Solomon would be the one to lead me back. I would find myself again and maybe even some meaning in my life. The sun was starting to come up and as I looked out my window to the coffee shop across the street, I saw Solomon looking up at me, and smiling. I smiled back and nodded. And at that moment, I knew hope again; hope that had vacated my mind and soul many months ago. I felt some of the old confidence come back, but this time it felt more grounded in something I did not understand, something more substantial than self-reliance based on ability or intelligence.

Confident that Solomon would be there when I needed him, I took my time in the shower. The warm, nourishing water rejuvenated me and seemed to cleanse the venom of the night before. Although it was my body that was being washed clean, I felt that my mind was experiencing the same thing at a level beyond my comprehension. I dressed with a surety that this day was somehow different than any other day of my life. I walked across the street without even looking, a sense of invulnerability washing over me.

"Being a bit cocky today, are we?" Solomon said, with that same smile and twinkle in his eye that I had come to know, however briefly.

"The usual?" I asked, with a joyful sense of familiarity with this very special man that I had become blessed with knowing. He chuckled as if he sensed my blossoming hope and I left to order coffee.

"You owe me a buck fifty, old man," I said, as I set his cup down in front of him.

"I'll take it off your bill, you ingrate" he replied with a straight face, but betrayed by the smiling eyes. "You had quite a journey last night, my young friend" he spoke after the requisite moments of stillness. "You almost did it, didn't you? But now you're here, and you have chosen to live."

"Solomon, whose voice was it I heard across the void?" I said, knowing that he was waiting for me to ask the question.

"It was the Son of God, Michael. It was you."

Damn, this man never ceased to amaze me. "Okay, if you say so. But make up your mind, was it the Son of God or was it me?" I said, half in jest.

"They are one in the same. Haven't you figured out that the separation we perceive with our physical senses is just illusion? Even the scientific world now understands that through the study of quantum physics. In fact, there has even been a movie made about it. And if it's on the silver screen and science knows it, it must be true," he finished, with that now familiar *poking fun at the world* look.

It must have been the blank look in my eyes that showed him that I didn't get it. This was just a bit too much to digest over coffee. "You will grasshopper," he joked in obvious reference to one of my favorite deceased TV shows, Kung Fu. "You will." We both laughed out loud with an abandon that brought smiles and laughter to our coffee house comrades. "Let's walk," said Solomon.

We strolled quietly across the street and onto the sidewalk above the seawall. I could have sworn that I saw that little old man skip at one point. Out of the blue, a skateboarder almost ran us down but Solomon never moved as the slender, shirtless teenage boy whizzed past him by the smallest of margins. In fact, he showed no signs of it even happening. I, on the other hand, was ready to kick the kid's butt but Solomon never lost his composure or the sense of calm that seemed to permeate everything he did. I started to ask him why the incident didn't faze him but something inside seemed to say that it just didn't matter. As I looked back from following the kid with my eyes, I noticed that Solomon had moved on toward the beach. I stepped up the pace and caught up to him just as we hit the warm, white sand.

"Michael, I'm going to give you the answer to all of your problems. That answer is conveyed in one word, *forgiveness*."

"Did you say *forgiveness*?" I responded.

"Yes, *forgiveness*. That will be one thousand dollars. Would you like to pay in cash, check, or VISA?"

"Huh?" was about all I could muster, the sly smile on his face escaping me for the moment.

"Okay, so you don't quite get it. But you will. Let's keep working on it," he said, still unable to keep from smiling at me like a wise old sage talking to some adolescent who thinks he knows everything but doesn't really have a clue.

Recovering, I said, "For a thousand bucks, do you think you could at least explain what you meant by that first statement?"

"Absolutely, my young friend. *Forgiveness* is letting go of everything that you know is not true. Releasing all that junk sets you free. Freedom allows you to be your true self. And that *True Self* has no problems."

"Okay then," I replied, as I reached for my wallet, pulling out my platinum VISA card and extending it to him. We both started laughing so hard I could have sworn I saw pelicans stop in mid-air. I felt so light from it, so free. I looked again at the pelicans in their effortless flight and saw there a glimpse of the freedom of not being attached to anything. I couldn't imagine how a pelican could have any problems.

"See what I mean?" Solomon said, interrupting my reverie. I turned to see him watching the pelicans with a sublimely contented smile on his face. "Time to think my young brother, time to ask your inner pelican to tell you the truth." Again, we both burst out laughing and in that moment, I realized how much I had come to admire this old man. I looked directly into his eyes for a brief moment, seeing that love reflected there, and then quickly looked away. I was embarrassed but was aware that Solomon was giving me something very precious, something I simply did not understand but still valued. I looked up at him to see him looking at me the way I had looked at my son the time he had discovered his first treasure.

"I need to go now Solomon," I half whispered, overcome by the memory and love for my son and my newfound friend and counselor.

"I know. See you tomorrow for coffee," he replied gently. And I left, leaving Solomon on the beach, watching the pelicans.

I couldn't decide what had made the most impact on me; Solomon's words or the effect of watching the pelicans gliding over the waves. There was a truth expressed by these birds that reached beyond words, or even thoughts. It seemed to reach inside me and touch something that knew that kind of freedom and effortless being. Solomon had said that forgiveness would set me free and then I had somehow experienced that sense of freedom watching the pelicans. Life had felt so heavy and arduous to me for so long that I was beginning to assimilate the weight as a part of my life. And then in an instant, I was reminded of a lightness that I never knew existed. But even as I now remember those dark moments, I can feel the heaviness returning. I had tasted the light and the thought of going back to the persistent and familiar darkness of recent months now seemed ominous. The day had exhausted me and my thoughts faded to black. What was it Solomon had said about *a True Self*?

Digesting Pelicans

Lanky birds soaring effortlessly
Skimming wave tops at peak
Reminding of something forgotten
Refusing to let me speak
Still filling my soul with wonder
Disarming demons at bay
The aged voice urges me on
Hoping I will longer stay
With ancient words of wisdom
So far above my brain
Words truly fit for consumption
Leading me home again

Naked at the Window

The morning sun streaming though my open window woke me from a dreamless sleep. I had the sense that something had happened but with no remembrance of what. In fact, I distinctly remembered not dreaming. I had been thinking of what Solomon had said to me about a *True Self* and then I woke up several hours later. All I knew was that I had experienced something yesterday that I wanted, no needed, to know more about. I got up and walked over to the window and then stopped short, realizing the window was open and I was naked. Sleeping in the nude was a long time habit; a way of feeling uninhibited, uncovered, and hiding nothing. In short, it was a small slice of freedom that I had allowed myself, cloistered within the boundaries of career and family. Something urged me to go to the window and just stand there unfettered by the trappings of acceptability. How free it would feel, just to stand there naked, unconcerned, and unrestrained. So I did! And it felt really great, at least until the thought of being arrested for public lewdness crept in and abruptly ended my birth-like joy of being naked in front of the world again. I thought, *how absurd that we cover our bodies when the shame is in our mind; a shame born of who knows what and for what reason*? We seemed to be so completely ruled by ideas and concepts that make no sense, imprisoned by our own guilt and fear. Could this *True Self* that Solomon mentioned and that seemed to be trying to take up residence in my head be the answer? After all, he had said it was free and it had no problems. How could it have no problems and still be prisoner to guilt and fear? Questions, nothing but questions. But the little old man sitting across the street had answers and I needed some; coffee, a toasted bagel, and answers. The thought of all three propelled me through my morning ritual and out the door to my now favorite coffee house.

Again, I dashed across the street with barely a glance. I had better pay more attention or one of these days I could wind up as spiritually evolved road kill. And there was Solomon, shaking his head and laughing at my carelessness.

"We better accelerate your sessions so I can get paid before you move on to greener, or should I say flatter, pastures," he declared, as I arrived at our usual table.

"Hey, pelicans don't stop for traffic, why should I?"

"Pelicans are free, and they can fly. Are you free Michael?"

Deflated by his comment, I muttered back, "No, I guess not, not yet anyway."

"Buy me a coffee my soon-to-be-free, traffic-ignoring, young pelican and we'll see what we can do about it. And one of Lisa's chocolate Danish please. I've developed quite an appetite watching you play dodgem cars." The mini bout with depression ended as suddenly as it had come on as I couldn't help but laugh at this man who seemed to be so confident and at peace with everything.

"You got it, old man. I'll *fly* right in and get that for you." Solomon raised his eyebrows as if to remind me to leave the puns to those of more subtle persuasion. As I returned with the food and drink, I thought I had spilled the coffee on Solomon. In fact, I could swear that the coffee tipped, left the cup, and then returned to equilibrium, all in a split second. Obviously, imitating pelicans and dodging cars was playing with my mind, or he was.

"How did that just happen?" I asked, dumbfounded.

"Sit the coffee down, and I'll tell you. I'm not sure we'll be so lucky the next time," he replied.

"Is that what it was, luck? Are you trying to tell me that the cup just righted itself because of luck?"

"Do you believe in luck, Michael? Or do you believe in reality?"

"I'm not really sure what you mean by either one of those terms. *Luck* is indefinable and *reality* is subjective. We each have our own version of both," I explained, in what I considered a rather insightful response.

"I apologize for having to burst your little bubble of new age awareness, but you're wrong on both counts. Luck is a label for something we don't understand and reality is not subjective. Reality is by definition, absolute. Illusion is subjective."

"Okay, I can buy the *luck* thing. But if reality is absolute as you say and we all experience the world differently, what does that say about our concept of reality?"

"Well, my young friend, I think you just answered your own question. If something is true, would it not be true in all cases and to all perceivers? If a thing is partially true, is it not also false and doesn't that paradox disqualify it from being true, by definition? Perhaps what we perceive with our senses is simply a very interesting, sometimes entertaining, and often terrifying, dream. In our nocturnal dreams, we can conjure it any way we want and, while in it, we believe it to be real. But when we awake, we realize that it has simply been a dream and we have made it all up in our minds. Is it possible that what we refer to as *reality* is simply another level of dreaming, one that we have yet to awaken from?"

"Holy crap old man, hold the boat. I'm still working on the True Self, free-the-pelican thing. Now you're trying to tell me this is all a dream?"

"Yes I am. And as you can see, in this particular place, a quite lovely one. But as you also know, it can just as well be as nightmarish as losing someone you love dearly. So the question becomes; do you want to keep the dream, or do you want to be free of it?"

"So what's on the other side of the dream?"

"Let's walk, and maybe your inner pelican will speak to us again," he said, eyes grinning.

Naked at the Window

*Naked I yearn to be
A baby once more and innocent
No restrictions for being free
Careless, aimless, just being
All I was meant to be
I know the truth is simple
This world cannot be true
Father, please help me overlook it
To witness and see only You*

Wisdom by the Sea

"Solomon, you told me yesterday that forgiveness would make me free and that freedom would allow me to be my True Self. Does that person reside in the dream?"

"When your True Self entertained the thought of separation from the oneness of God, the mind split. It split into one side that believed it was possible to be apart from its source, its Creator, and another side that knew it was inconceivable to leave. The separated side was instantaneously overcome with a sense of guilt at betraying its Creator and fear of retaliation for having done so. The side that remained true to its Source knew that the thought of betrayal was possible only in a separated mind and that God's love for his creation would never allow retaliation. God is love my friend, and love by its very nature unifies and finds separation incomprehensible. The separated part of the mind has been called by many names; the devil, Satan, or in psychological terms, the ego. The True Self that remained in oneness with God is His Son."

"So this person is the Son of God, the one we refer to as Christ?"

"Yes, and it is not a person or a body or a thing. It is mind and it is spirit. And it is that core of your being that will someday make you free; free of the world and all the problems that the thought of separation brings."

"Why do you keep referring to it as the *thought* of separation instead of just the separation?" I asked, thinking I had finally tripped him up.

"Because the separation is not real. The separated self became enamored with the *thought* of separation and made it its reality. But since separated oneness can't possibly be real, it was necessary to make a world that reinforced our belief in it. In this world, we see what we want to believe and then we believe what we see. That circular form of perception locks us into the *seeming* reality of what is essentially an illusion, or a dream. Why do you think there are so many contradictions, opposites, and conflicting viewpoints in the world? The world is inherently false. It is based on the separation from truth and the notion that we can survive without the Source of all there is. We have been in the dream for so long now that we have forgotten that it is a dream. It has become our reality."

"So once again, Michael I ask you, do you want the dream; the dream where your boy dies from a bullet in his head from his so-called best friend, the dream where you seriously considered doing the same to yourself?"

I stood there dumbfounded and then it all came crashing down on me again; the grief, the loss, the anger, the hatred, the depression, and wanting to die rather than face another day. And standing there on the beach, I wept. I cried so hard, I dropped to my knees and my heavy heart felt like it would sink into a bottomless ocean. I sat there crying until I was empty, until I could cry no more. Solomon gently put his hand on my head and we sat in silence; watching the sea, and the sun, and the pelicans.

Wisdom by the Sea

*So long have I believed
All that I was taught to believe
No reason to challenge or deny
Hard to accept this notion of reality
Yet difficult to let it go by
Then I ponder what Christ would do
Instead of a living a lie
Can it be but wishful thinking
That leads me to think otherwise
Or could a holy, peaceful world
Be hiding behind the lie
There may be some need
To destroy that which bids me blind
In order to see quite farther
To find the truth inside*

The Sink Hole

I LEFT SOLOMON YESTERDAY still sitting on the beach as the sun went down over the Pacific. After several hours of sitting in complete silence, I had arisen without saying a word and walked slowly back to the Inn. Walking back, I realized that I had let go of a huge weight, a burden I had carried ever since Chris died. I was emotionally raw but felt cleansed and much lighter. Was it possible the grief was gone or had I just temporarily purged myself emotionally? I guess time would tell but, if nothing else, I had slept like a baby. As I lay here in my bed feeling the cool ocean breezes flowing over me, I cannot help but wonder where all this is going, where this wise old man is taking me. I have less will to spring out of bed this morning, less enthusiasm but more peace. A sense of calm acceptance has come over me but I also know there is much to learn, and learn I will. My dear counselor has touched me in a way I never knew was possible and I anticipate it will change my life in ways I can't yet imagine.

Oddly, I halt at the edge of the street on my way to the coffee house. It's not that I'm afraid or even concerned about getting run over. I think I now value my life more than I did before and it seems too important to be careless with it. Solomon watches me from across the street, this time without the grin but more with a look of affection.

"Good morning, I see you slept well," he said generously, as I approached.

"I did Solomon. I certainly did."

"Michael, please sit. I believe it is my turn to get the refreshments." He pointed to the chair and asked "The usual?"

"Just coffee this morning, I don't have much of an appetite."

"Coming up, my young friend," he said, his hand resting lightly on my shoulder as he passed. He somehow knew that it was gentleness I needed. The banter would have to wait. We drank our coffee in relative quiet, mainly watching the sea and the early surfers heading towards the jetty with their long boards underarm. After awhile, Solomon stood and said "The sea beckons and we have much to talk about." I nodded and we left.

As my bare feet touched the now familiar white sand and the warmth of it comforted me, I felt like I was melting into it. It seemed like I could just keep sinking farther and farther if I would just agree to. The world would simply swallow me if I let it, but I knew it was my choice and I had the power to consent or decline the offer.

"Tempting, isn't it?" I heard Solomon say from in front, still with his back to me.

"How did you know?" I replied, emerging from the spiritual sink hole.

"The world is a very seductive place, grasshopper. We have made it so attractive that we will even tolerate its pain and suffering, at least until it becomes unbearable. For you, it has become so. You are now ready to learn the way out and it is my responsibility, and honor, to be your guide."

"I am the one who is honored Solomon."

"Let's talk about *forgiveness*" he said, briefly lowering his eyes in acknowledgement of my compliment. Before I could respond, a dolphin breaking the water and sailing through the air drew my attention. And right behind the first came a second, and then a third.

"Did you see that?' I said excitedly. And of course he had, as I turned to see him watching intently.

"The Holy Spirit sends us many signs, if we are awake enough to see them, or hear them," he replied, still watching the dolphins as they continued to surf the waves in perfect unison. "Mostly symbols; words are so limited and so easily misinterpreted. So what do you think the dolphins symbolize?"

"As Don McLean once wrote '*The three men I admire the most; the Father, Son, and the Holy Ghost*" I responded, not knowing where the bit of rhyme came from. I did not plan it, but I knew it was true.

"Excellent, my young brother, excellent!" he exclaimed, as he turned and smiled. "Enough for today, go and dream about dolphins. And ask for more understanding. Tomorrow, we'll talk about forgiveness. The Holy Spirit does not abide by the plans of men." And once again I left him standing on the beach, still gazing and smiling at the blue Pacific and its glorious attendants.

The Sink Hole

Pearls of wisdom lightly strewn
Through fertile ground of mind
Consuming each as given
Good fruit for the soul to find
Words can do love no justice
Even symbols may not be true
But know we will when truth but knocks
And tells us what we must do
So change my mind, I will
My soul does beckon it so
Learn to live a better way
Than life has shown me to go
I accept the truth when presented
I know it from impeccable faith
Let this messenger sent to me lately
Be the one to deliver my fate

Re-living the Past

After leaving Solomon, I had walked around the village for awhile, ate a quiet dinner, and retired early. So much had happened and I needed time to understand it all. And I did dream of dolphins; beautiful, graceful dolphins. I awoke around 3am and went to the bathroom to relieve myself; all those of dreams of water, I guess. I looked into the mirror and I was smiling. Either the dreams were better than I thought or Solomon's ever-present smile was becoming contagious. For being that early, I did feel pretty damn good. These few past days had given me some of the best sleep I had in months and I was starting to feel more optimistic about where I was headed.

Some of my earliest experiences with religion weren't very positive. The first church my parents took me to ended up being one of the most humiliating experiences of my life when the pastor singled me out to come forward and repent. Hell, I didn't even know I had done anything wrong. I was very shy as a kid and spent most of my time inside my own head. Being embarrassed like that at an early age and in front of so many people frightened and scarred me. Fortunately, my parents were as turned off by the incident as I was and we never went back. Years later, my family became interested in Catholicism and eventually I was *encouraged* to take catechism lessons and be baptized. I enjoyed the rituals and the beauty of the Latin language but soon became disillusioned by the emphasis on money. It seemed to my young mind that the church was more concerned with raising funds than they were with saving souls. So after a few years of attending Mass on a quasi-compulsory basis, I managed to lessen my involvement and eventually quit going to church altogether.

Although most organized religion soon ceased to have any appeal to me, I nevertheless continued to pursue *spiritual* studies on my own. I was intrigued by the studies of psychology, philosophy, meditation, and spiritual practices like Buddhism. I read the Edgar Cayce books, the Carlos Castaneda adventures, and anything else I could get my hands on concerning the human mind and spirit. And although it was all very interesting, including a period of checking out the new age stuff in the seventies, it all seemed to fall short of explaining the true nature of life for me.

I was eventually seduced by the good old American pursuit of materialism and started putting my education, intelligence, and inquisitiveness to work chasing the almighty buck. Along with a successful career in the technology arena and a steep rise up the corporate ladder, I also managed to squeeze in a marriage to a great woman and father three great kids. One of those children was my only son Chris, and his untimely and violent death at the tender age of seventeen turned my life upside down. And from there, I find myself here in sunny southern California, dreaming about dolphins. So how does a maverick ex-mystic with a BMW and a six-figure salary derive meaning from three surfing dolphins?

When Solomon had asked me what I thought the dolphin show meant, without thinking, the lyrics of the classic rock hit *American Pie* came into my head and I blurted it out as if it were the most natural thing in the world to say. But why would a reformed catholic equate three mammalian surfers to the Holy Trinity? My disillusionment with religion had likely caused me to *throw out the baby with the bath water,* so to speak. I knew my entire life that I believed in a divine Creator but I guess I also believed in his created Son and the Holy Spirit that tries to reach us in this materialistic world. I think they all just want to see us return home. So was the Holy Spirit showing me symbolically that what I needed to heal my soul was the Father, the Holy Spirit, and his Son? And was, as Solomon said, the Son me? I knew I wasn't Jesus or Buddha, or any other great historical Messiah, but I felt that God *was* my true Father. And if He was my Creator, He must be the Creator and Father to all of us. So how could that be if he only had one Son? Solomon said that the separation we see everywhere in this world was an illusion. So maybe we are all His *One Son*, one with our Creator and each other, but trapped in this dream of separated beings.

He had also asked me if I wanted to know *reality*. Did he mean this reality, the reality of God and Spirit? And if so, didn't that preclude the things we could see or hear or touch from being true or real? How could a world of hatred, violence, guilt, and conflict be real if we truly believed in a loving Father? He would never create a world like this for his beloved children, so who did? Maybe, as Solomon has indicated, *we did*. In our dreams! Maybe we got lost in a dream and forgot where we belonged. Well crap, more questions and no answers. So after pondering these questions for some time, I showered, dressed, and headed for the caffeine cathedral across the street for some answers.

"So, my religiously challenged apprentice, it seems you had quite a little conversation with yourself this morning. I was afraid you would figure it all out on your own and I would have to find a real job."

"One of these days, you're going to have to tell me how you know all these things without me telling you," I responded, as I gestured drinking coffee on my way into the café. He nodded, I bought. I returned with the usual straight coffee for Solomon, a chocolate pastry he didn't ask for but I knew he wanted, and a double espresso for my rattled brain.

"Thank you, kind sir. You're a scholar and a gentleman. Not much of a catholic, but a passable servant."

"Hey, a servant I'm not. You can get your own damn coffee next time," I said, with some repartee of my own.

"Never think that, my friend," he replied. "The best we can be is a servant to each other. It's the only way we'll ever get out of this mess we made," he said, in a rare bit of early morning seriousness.

"Noted," I affirmed, understanding fully what he meant. "Well Solomon, I think I understand what the dolphins were saying to me yesterday. I consulted my inner pelican last night and all was revealed to me. Well maybe not *all*, but a boatload of interesting questions sure popped up."

"Yes, and you already know the answers to them, don't you? The questions were the answers as well. Everything you surmised is true and the dolphins were simply a mechanism to trigger your ancient memories. Now that you understand that this world is indeed illusion and our true reality is waiting for us beyond the dream, you are ready, like the prodigal son, to learn how to return home."

"Forgiveness, right?"

"Your learning is accelerating now that you have allowed the Holy Spirit to participate in your life," he said to me in a soft voice, as if it were too sacred to allow the world to hear.

"I've allowed *you* to participate in my life Solomon. And in case I forget, thank you."

"It's all the same, remember? And believe me, you won't forget. You haven't seen my bill yet." We both laughed and I knew that anything that felt this good and this right and this joyful had to have come from a divine source.

"Shall we see what wonders the sea holds for us today my dear friend?" I said, almost overwhelmed by the fineness of the moment.

"Let's," he said. And once again, we headed towards that vast expanse of wonderful sand and ocean I had come to cherish.

Re-living the Past

*Before me stands on principle
A man of impeccable timing
An angel sent from Paradise
A being of enjoyable rhyming
Employed to make us think twice
Concerning the world about us
Whether it be pleasure or vice
It doesn't really matter, he says
It's all a matter of time
Before we begin to see clearly
And put it all behind
Permitted now to approach the way
Cleared to make dreams unwind*

Forgiveness 101

The feel of the sand was exquisite between my toes as we walked in silence along the water's edge. "You know Solomon, I've come to love this place."

"Don't get too attached. It's beautiful no doubt, but it's still an illusion. Where we're going eventually will make this place look like south central LA after a Ku Klux Klan rally," he said smiling, obviously amusing himself with his analogy.

"Riots and cross burning aside, I plan on enjoying it as along as I can," I said.

"Absolutely, no other way to go. Enjoy everything in life. That's what God intended for us until we blew it with our little act of rebellion. Just don't get too attached and forget that it's the same world that killed Christopher." My heart flinched at the mention of Chris. It hurt less than before, but it still hurt.

"Solomon, why so much pain and why do I feel so guilty about Chris?" I found myself asking him, surprised that I had done so.

"That's why we're here; to give you the key to healing your pain, dissolving your guilt, and losing your fear."

"I didn't say I was afraid," I defended, feeling it was wrong as soon as I said it. Solomon just looked at me, knowing that a response was unnecessary.

"Today, we start your learning and your healing. Today you start forgiving."

"Teach me old wise and ancient one," I said, as I bowed to him in quasi-mock reverence.

"*Wise*, I can live with but if you don't drop the *ancient* routine, you're going to see exactly how much those bombardier seagulls love me," he joked. At least I hoped he was joking, this was a brand new shirt.

Solomon looked longingly and quietly at the endless azure sky for what seemed like an eternity and then turned to me saying, "The first thing

Forgiveness 101

to know about *forgiveness* is that you forgive *nothing*." Then he stopped and went back to staring at the heavens.

I waited for him to continue and when he showed no signs of doing so, I responded, "Is that it? Hell, I can forgive *nothing* in my sleep. So do I pay up now?" But none of my sarcasm moved him at all. I wasn't quite sure what to do next, so I did nothing. I waited.

"I don't mean *nothing* in the sense that there is no one or no thing to forgive. We forgive nothing because all of the so-called sins we prescribe to ourselves and others, all of the things we think we do to hurt each other, and all of the imagined slights, are just that, *imagined*."

"So if one of your seagulls poops on my shoulder, it's just my imagination?"

"To be technically correct, actually they're *projected*, not imagined," he said, a wry smile trying to escape his face.

"Well now you're talking like the psychotherapist I thought you were when Wayne sent me to you. So does this mean the price goes up? Last time I heard, the hourly rate for a sage was a lot less than a shrink."

"The price is the same, my young friend. The price is nothing. You pay nothing, you forgive nothing. Everything that you judge or condemn someone for, including yourself, is a projection of guilt from your ego mind."

"But if it's from my mind, isn't it still real, not *nothing*?" I responded.

"Guilt will seem real to you because you believe you need it. You think you need it because when we *seemingly* separated from God, we thought we had committed the screw-up of the millennium. Imagine for just a moment how it would have felt to believe you had just thrown away everything and betrayed your Creator and the Source of all life. That moment was the birth of guilt and fear in our minds. That fear and guilt *drove us out of the garden*, out of the Heaven and oneness of our divine minds."

"Man, that's one helluva concept," I replied. For the first and only time, an infinitesimal moment, I saw sadness flicker in Solomon's eyes, and then vanish just as quickly.

"It's not a concept, Michael. It is truth and it was the saddest day in eternity."

I didn't know what to say. I understood in my own limited way but even a hint of remorse and sadness of that magnitude was too much to ponder. "I'm sorry, Solomon." He said nothing for what seemed like forever. He finally turned away from the sky and the ocean and looked at me.

"Let's stop for today, my friend," and he turned and walked away.

Forgiveness 101

The place we left, the Home we lost
On that sad and mournful day
Came to exit a mind with none
Yet free to believe it or stay
The celestial apple bitten
Tasting awareness of separation
Rode the wave of illusion
To a place of major confusion
Left the garden gate wide open
The Gatekeeper kept it that way
To await our eventual return
Sad it was but not eternal
Lost for quite some time
Yet angels sent to find us
Return us home to Heaven
Back to One some day

Practice Makes Perfect

A VOICE, BOTH GENDERLESS and infinitely gentle, woke me from my slumber. It seemed to come from inside my mind but it was clearly not my voice and it didn't even seem to be my thought. The voice said *"There is nothing to fear,"* and that was all. I didn't know whether to savor the moment or eject out of bed and go for cover. But the voice was so comforting and it felt so natural and safe, that I just lay there with my heart pounding and my eyes wide open in awe.

After awhile, I got up and walked to the window, this time fearlessly naked, and looked across the street to the café. Solomon was not there! For a moment, I panicked. I guess I had come to take it for granted that he would always be there, sitting in that same chair, at that same table, waiting for me to join him. What had happened to him, where was he? And once again, the voice repeated *"There is nothing to fear,"* and instantly I was calm and at peace. The peace that came over me was unlike anything I had ever experienced in my life. It was profound. And in that first moment of serenity, I knew that Solomon was at the beach waiting for me and that the voice was somehow his. It didn't sound like his voice at all, but I knew it was. I dressed, skipping the mandatory shower that I rarely missed, and walked downstairs past the café and straight to the beach.

The Carlsbad beach is pretty long but without seeing him, I walked down the seawall and down to the beach directly to where Solomon was, without so much as a wasted step. "You're late," he said, as I approached, smiling of course.

"Well it wasn't like you left me precise directions, you know," I bantered back.

"*Au contraire*, my young psychic. I left you very precise directions. Do you see now what is possible in the reality of the mind, the *One Mind*? Direct, instantaneous communication is just one of the many treasures of the Mind. Someday, we will all understand how primitive our communication here is and how natural it is when we remember that we all share the same Mind and Spirit."

"You never cease to amaze me Solomon," I responded, still dumbfounded by the wisdom of this excellent soul.

"Consider it a bonus, a freebie if you will. But while you're so busy being impressed, remember that we are the same, you and I. The only difference is that I *know* that. No one of us is special but we are all divine. And trust me, divine is better."

"All righty then, what else do you have for me today? I'm getting a little bored with the parlor tricks," and we both laughed.

"Today, we work. Today, you start forgiving. Today is the hard part."

"So you mean I actually have to apply all this wisdom you been throwing at me for the past week?" I said, half serious, half joking, half afraid.

"We're going to start with an easy one. Who did you love the most between your parents?"

"I suppose that would be my mother. I wanted to love my dad more but he kept me at a distance most of the time. Too busy working all the time, don't you know."

"You mean like you did with your children?" he replied.

"I guess so Solomon, I guess so," as my mood flattened.

"That subject is for another day my young friend. But I want you to feel that loss. It will help you to forgive your dad. You know that you never intentionally, or should I say consciously, kept your children at bay. And neither did your dad. In fact, your dad did nothing to you, just like you did nothing to your children. You took your self-inflicted guilt over *betraying* your Holy Father and projected it onto your dad. Neither one of you deserved it. You never betrayed your Father and your dad never betrayed you. Know that the guilt you prescribed to your dad and to yourself is false. It is unreal and it is the separated mind's way of keeping you separate not only from your brothers and children, but from your Father as well."

"So what do I do Solomon?" I said, my sadness deepening.

"Forgive your dad for what he did not do. Let go of the guilt that you put on him and just love him."

"But he's dead. How I can I tell him I forgive him? He died knowing I was angry at him."

"*Is* he dead, Michael? Is the *reality* the world and the body or is it God and his one eternal Son?"

I knew he was right, and unexpectedly I blurted out "I forgive you, dad. You never hurt me and I know that now. I love you and we're okay." And in that moment of truth, I let go of the anger, resentment, and grief that I had felt for my dad.

"That's enough for one day. Give yourself time to let it heal and feel the freedom of forgiveness." Solomon then hugged me, smiled, and laid his hand on my shoulder. And then he left me to be alone.

I thought a lot about my dad after that. I walked to a nearby park and sat on the grass, remembering all the good times we had when I was a kid and how we had then somehow drifted apart as I got older. As I let myself go back to that time, thoughts other than what my dad had *done* to me began to surface. I started to remember what a pain in the ass I was as a teenager. The sarcastic remarks, the times I blew him off when he asked me to do things that I considered too juvenile, and the moments when I could see in his eyes he wanted to hug me and I just looked or walked away. I guess it hadn't all been about him working all the time. Maybe he worked all the time because he didn't feel wanted at home. I thought about the times Chris had done similar things to me and how it had hurt like hell, and how it made me want to close up and just go away.

So if I looked at those things from my dad's perspective, I could understand why he wasn't around so much, why he seemed to want to be somewhere else so much of the time. So maybe this forgiveness idea was just a matter of looking at things from a different perspective, walking a mile in his shoes. And as I was laying there looking up at the cerulean sky feeling rather pleased with myself and my new insights, I heard the voice again. "*There is nothing to forgive.*" I was jolted out of my smugness and almost out of my shorts! Here I was thinking I had finally figured it all out and this voice was telling me I was dead wrong. I had just come to the conclusion that what my dad had done was justified and therefore I forgave him for his failings as a father. Now, I wasn't so sure. This was all getting pretty confusing and I decided to wait until tomorrow and ask Solomon about it.

Practice Makes Perfect

*Rest assured dear cynic
There is much evidence to approve
The darkness carried in mind
Murder us it will
If left to its own device
Best given to another
To let our sin become their vice
Yet truly innocent we all must be
Created by perfect hands
Residing still in perfect Mind
No need to pardon or forgive
The nothing we never committed
Except in illusion denied*

Just Another Day at the Beach

As the two of us settled in again at our favorite table, I could hardly wait to ask Solomon about my latest revelation. Just as I was getting ready to raise the subject, he said, "So you want to know why you were wrong about your dad?"

"Solomon, will you please, just one time, allow me to ask my own damn questions?"

"Of course I will. Why didn't you just say so? I was trying to save you some time and as you know, time is money," he said, with that same mischievous grin that he had when he was making fun of me. "Would you like to restate the question in your own terms?"

"No, but in the future I would like to voice my own thoughts before you do if you don't mind," I stated, without a lot of conviction.

"Certainly. Now would you like my answer or do you want to handle that one yourself? You do have the answer already, in case you didn't know. But, since I also know that you don't know that yet, I'll field this one," he ended, mercifully. "The reason you were wrong about your dad is that you forgave him for something he never did. Just because you believe you know what he was thinking and why doesn't mean it was real. Forgiving someone because you are now wise and benevolent enough to let go of their transgressions is simply making the so-called *sin* real. And sin is not real. It is not real because it happened only in a dream."

"I'll give you a good example," he continued. "Remember early on in your marriage to Grace when she would have dreams of you being unfaithful?" I nodded, remembering the frustration of defending something I hadn't done. "Do you remember how she would wake up angry at you and then forgive you once she realized it was just a dream? She was, in essence, forgiving you for something you had never done but in that brief moment before she was fully awake, it was real to her. You, my friend, are not yet fully awake and until you are, you will continue to believe that all of the things that happen in your dream are real. Perspectives are more or less clear but they are never wholly true. Perception is a tool the ego uses to confuse our minds and keep us separate. Using the unified Mind of the True Self takes us past the relativity of perception to the absoluteness of truth. Your perception of your dad's reality was just another facet of the dream and a projection of your mind's guilt onto him. Forgive him not because he had good reasons for his actions but instead because they never actually happened."

"Okay, I guess I'm just living the dream," I replied, halfway trying to be funny and halfway trying to assimilate what he was saying to me. "You realize it's not that easy to grasp the idea that all of this is just a dream or illusion?"

"Yes, I do. If it were easy, we wouldn't have been stuck here for so long. But think about it for a moment Michael. We both know that you experimented with hallucinogenics in your earlier days. Don't you remember how real those illusions seemed while you were in them? How much you believed in them, even to the point of acting on those beliefs? People have jumped out of windows believing they could fly while on LSD. And countless people have committed suicide based on some *belief* about their life that was real only to them. We see what we believe and then we believe what we see. The problem is that we see with a divided mind that is incapable of knowing what is true. So we all go around seeing the world in different ways, never realizing that it is all crap!"

"Solomon, I'm appalled. You just called the world *crap*."

"I did, and compared to the real world, the world of unified Mind and Spirit, it truly is. You may have some good times in your life but as long as you believe in the world of separation, you will also have conflict, pain, and suffering. I cannot because I know it is not in the nature of the Divine to be so and I choose to live in my True Self and therefore in the One Mind and Spirit. Freedom from this world is possible, revealing the gifts our Father has always intended for us, the only ones that really matter."

"And that freedom comes from forgiveness, right? The kind of forgiveness that realizes that nothing true or real has been done to us, and therefore simply lets it go?"

"Yes my brother, yes!" his face radiating as he grabbed me by both arms and squeezed. "Now you have it. Let's call it a day and tomorrow we'll practice on your mother." And then that little old man just took off running down the beach. About fifty yards away, he suddenly leapt into the air, flapped his arms, and made a sound I could have sworn was a pelican.

Just Another Day at the Beach

Forgive me Father for I have sinned
Falser words were never spoken
Children of God could be but perfect
Even if thoughts are broken
Freedom and free will gave us leave
To choose what never could be
We can think of imperfection
Yet by nature we cannot be
Lost and confused may be our hell
But we may never leave
The Source of all that created us
Forgiven for a dream our reprieve

Hot Java

Back at the café the next morning, Solomon and I greeted each other without words. I sat down at our table immediately as he had already retrieved the coffee. Assuming it would be getting cold, I took a big gulp. The startled and pained look on my face triggered a bout of laughter from Solomon.

"What the hell, Solomon!" I screeched. "You could have told me it was still hot."

"But it would not have been nearly as much fun as watching you get angry at yourself and instantly blaming it on me," he replied, partially diffusing my rage.

"Okay, so it was my own fault. I should have tested it first."

"It's very human Michael to project our own guilt onto others and then become indignant and angry about it. What you just experienced was a mini-lesson in how that works. You felt stupid for making an assumption that wasn't what you expected, followed by the shame of having blown your perfectionist cover. Since we don't like to feel our guilt because it takes us too close to the pain of separation, we instantly project it onto someone else and find ways to justify our anger over what we *think* they have done to us. It's the thing that starts everything from marital spats to wars. It just depends on who's running the projector."

"That's a lot of philosophizing over a hot cup of coffee, don't you think?" I asked.

"Remember the pelicans and the dolphins? The Holy Spirit teaches us in many ways," he replied.

"Point taken," I said, feeling a bit stupid, *again*. But as the anger started welling up in me I realized what he meant and I chose, in that moment, not to justify my anger and not to give it any energy.

"Well done," Solomon replied, in obvious reference to my decision even though I had not voiced it. I was becoming used to him knowing what I was thinking and I was now beginning to know a little about his mind as well.

"You can drink your coffee now. I believe all that huffing and puffing has cooled it down," he said, smiling, still digging for any remnants of my anger.

But I had beaten it; one small victory over my own separated mind. "Not today, Solomon. I get it." He nodded, smiled, and raised his cup in salutation.

"Shall we see what truth the oceans will bring us today, my young friend?"

"Indeed, Solomon," as I fearlessly gulped down the entire cup of coffee and mock slammed it down on the table. "To the sea, old salt, to the sea."

We walked side by side in silence as we always had, not speaking until the sand greeted our naked feet. And then Solomon declared, "You hated your mother, Michael."

I couldn't believe those words had come out of his mouth! The anger again surged and, for a moment, I hated him for accusing me of this unspeakable sin. I was so enraged I could not speak.

"You never thought you could hate me either but you do now," he replied, while I was still deciding how to rearrange his face. "We all hate, Michael. At least in that part of our mind that is separate from God. Just like we project our *guilt* onto others, we do the same with our hatred. It emerges from our own self-hate and that stems from how we felt when we thought that by abandoning our Creator we had given away everything for nothing."

Even though my anger was driving me to hurt him, his words somehow pierced the wall of my rage and started to calm me. I unclenched my fists and let the anger start to leave my mind.

"Good, my young friend, good," he said, in a way that further soothed and comforted me.

After finally regaining some composure, I said, "You took a hell of a chance with that statement Solomon. I loved my mother dearly and I wanted to rip your head off a minute ago. I'm much bigger and younger than you. Weren't you afraid?"

He laughed and said, "I replaced fear with love a long time ago my young would-be pugilist. I have no fear because I know that you, or anyone else for that matter, cannot harm me. I am not this body. I am Mind and I am Spirit and you cannot harm either of those. They are, as are we all, eternal. Only a mind *seemingly* separated from the Creator of all that is real could believe that it can harm the eternal. An illusion can be dispelled because it is not real but love is not affected in the slightest by anything unreal."

"So you were not intimidated in the least? What was your reaction?"

"Well, I was somewhat amused by the tirade and confident your True Self would come to your rescue."

"Well all I can say is I'm damn glad you weren't amused in front of the coffee shop," I said, smiling, as my old ally humor rejoined the party.

"I would have never done that, my friend. Adding guilt and shame to the mix might have been a bit much for you. But you did well. I hit a nerve and touched on something that you didn't want to look at, but now you do. Mission accomplished."

"So you really believe that I *hated* my mother?" I asked, almost choking on the words.

"Yes Michael. But you *loved* her far more. The ego hates, your True Self loves. There is no judgment attached. It's just a matter of which part of the mind you want to live in. We have all hated and most of us have loved during the many lives we have made for ourselves in the world. Do not condemn yourself. Ask the Holy Spirit to help you choose the right way for you."

"So how do I go about forgiving my mother?" I finally asked.

"No need to. You already know that anything that she may have done to invoke your hatred was your projection. There is simply nothing to forgive her for."

"So why all of this?" I said. "Why even bring it up?" I asked, in bewilderment.

"So that you could forgive *yourself* and let go of the guilt you have harbored for hating her. Hating our parents brings us too close to how we feel about our one true parent and how we feel about ourselves for betraying Him. You needed to feel the anger in order to understand what lies beneath it."

"So how do I tell on my own when these emotions are so deeply buried?"

"Irritation, anger, and rage are all the same; varying only by degree and how much you want to let out. Anger is never justified in reality. Only the separated mind justifies it to itself so that it can self-righteously attack and thereby maintain separation. The True Self knows that anger, fear, and guilt are all just ways that the separated mind justifies its distinct existence from the One Mind and Spirit. If we are all truly one, which we are, then who do you attack, if not yourself?"

"But you didn't answer my question," I insisted.

"But I did. The presence of anger, irritation, guilt, or fear indicates that you have decided to use the separated mind instead of the True Self. You can spend a lot of time trying to figure out why or you can simply choose not to play there. What we give our energy to, grows. And that's as true of anger as it is for love. We have been in denial of truth for countless ages. It is time to deny what we know is *not* real and turn our attention to what is."

"So what's next, old wise one?"

"For today, nothing. Know that, in truth, you loved your mother and your dad and they both loved you. As before, there is simply nothing to forgive. Take some time and think about that. Tomorrow we get serious," he said, smiling, causing an instant chill to run up my spine.

Hot Java

The door has opened
The dove has been set free
Guilt, shame, and fear
Exposed for what they be
The chains that bind us
We don't even see
We can trust but One
He who loves us in purity
Who waits until we are done
And when that glorious day arrives
He will greet us at glory's gate
Happy at last to see us
Knowing we no longer wait
Revealing our one true fate

The Whale

I WRESTLED WITH MYSELF most of the night, moving from demon to demon in my dreams. It was hard to admit to myself that hate, fear, and guilt were in me. I had covered my feelings with such a layer of sophistication over the years that I had somehow convinced myself that I was above all of that. But I was forced to admit now that there was a part of me where these foul things lived. So how was all this affecting me now in my life? How did they come into play in my current bout between wanting to live or die? Maybe that was the *serious business* Solomon had referred to yesterday. I decided to just wait and see. Although my dreams had engendered more questions than answers, I did awake feeling at peace with both of my deceased parents. All I could feel now when I thought of them was love. Could it be as simple as recognizing how I truly felt and letting go of the now conscious negative thoughts and feelings?

Morning dawned and since more questions demanded more answers and more caffeine, I was off once again to my favorite buzz factory. Not as intense as the cocaine I had used to *up myself* occasionally after Chris' death, but the coffee house conversation more than compensated for it. Thinking back on those days that now seemed so distant, I wondered how I ever thought I could find salvation in a pile of white powder or at the bottom of a liquor glass. We spend so much of our lives digging ourselves into and out of holes, it's a wonder we have any time for attending our own spirit. But here I was, despite all the detours, enrolled in a sort of divine rehab, and the stakes was my soul.

But why live in the past when I had so much to learn. It was time to get back to work and the boss was waiting.

"Hi boss," I said, as I approached Solomon who was standing, talking to a group of very attentive people.

"I must go my friends. I need to put this young man to work so he can earn his keep." They all laughed and returned to their conversation as he turned towards me.

The Whale

"I thought I would stump you with the *boss* reference but, once again, you were too quick for me," I said, as we found our seats.

"Let's have our coffee and talk. That is unless you would rather indulge in a little nose candy?" he said.

"It's a damn good thing I don't mind you invading my thoughts," I replied, still in awe of his abilities.

"I have never *invaded* your thoughts Michael. You invited me even though you are not aware of it yet. We share the One Mind and you have decided that is where you want to be. Even before we met in the physical world, you asked me to be your guide and teach you the landscape."

"I apologize, Solomon. I think I knew that all along but it sure has been fun bitching about it with you. I believe it was Edgar Cayce who once said *that some forms of evil are so subtle that only humor can dispel them.* And we don't seem to have any shortage of that."

"Edgar Cayce was a great soul and he knew of what he spoke. He was referring to our tendency to take our separated selves too seriously and being able to laugh at ourselves and the absurdity of the world is often our best way out. He also spoke of something he called the *Akashic Record* which was a reference to his perception of the One Mind that contains all thought. Many of our greatest teachers are discounted, ridiculed, and even ostracized in the world. The separated mind fears the messages they bring and knows that truth threatens its survival. But that's not why we're here today. Today we're here for another lesson in forgiveness."

"I agree. Besides, what did Cayce know? He was always sleeping on the job," I replied, unable to resist yet another pun. Solomon just smiled and shook his head.

"Let's go, I can't take it anymore," he replied, as he motioned towards the beach.

After our usual wordless journey to the beach, I couldn't help myself and said, "Solomon, since we always walk in silence until we make the beach, should we call this the *sands of silence*?"

"If you don't stop it my young would-be comic, I'm going to get inside your mind and erase everything I've told you. You're giving humor a bad name and I won't put up with it," he said, unable to smother the smile he was trying so hard to restrain.

"Okay, *uncle*. I know better than to piss you off. Let's talk forgiveness."

"Let's. I need a little myself after putting up with those horrible jokes." He reached out and put his hand on the side of my face. Then, without warning, he turned and pointed to a whale about hundred yards out from the beach. "They rarely come this close to shore. Pay attention Michael. This is for you."

"A whale just for me? I'm honored," I replied, in mock humility.

"No need for false humility, it's your whale. You put it there. Do you think it is harder to materialize a whale than it is to come back from the dead? You have done just that, my young disbeliever. And now, your True Self is trying to tell you something by projecting a whale for you to contemplate."

"So what is it trying to tell me?" I asked. I received no answer from the old guy as he just stood there watching the whale. "Solomon?"

"You tell me," he replied.

"Maybe it's telling me that I'm about to see something really *big*?"

"You're partially right, keep going," he prodded.

"The whale, like the pelicans and dolphins, roams free," I said, as the proverbial light bulb came on in my head. "Something big that will make me free? Is that it?" I asked, knowing as soon as I did that I was right. Solomon nodded, still with his back to me.

Half afraid to ask, I said, "Tell me Solomon."

After what seemed like an interminable pause, he spoke. "Christopher wants you to forgive his killer, Michael."

I could not speak. I simply could not make a sound. What was he asking me to do? Was he asking me to just let go of the fact that someone had placed a gun to the back of my son's head and pulled the trigger? Forgive the person who had taken my only son, my beautiful boy, from me at the age of seventeen? Forgive the one who ripped my heart out and drove any kind of meaning and joy from my life? I could not. I would not! I hate this damn kid and I want him to suffer like I've suffered.

"How can you ask this of me Solomon? Do you know what this kid did to me, my son, and my family?" I felt my rage turn to sadness so deep that I thought I would drown in it. "He killed my only son. He took my life away," I managed to utter weakly, as the grief once again threatened to overcome me.

"Chris isn't dead, Michael. Yes, the body is gone but he lives, now and forever."

The Whale

"Bullshit, Solomon. That little bastard killed my boy and you know it," the venom once again rising to the surface like dark red molten lava.

"He wants you to forgive his killer, not for his sake, and not even for Chris' sake. He wants you to forgive him for your sake. I know Chris. I know him even better than you do. He knows that no harm has been done him because he knows that who he is can never be harmed. His body was an illusion and now it's gone. He's happy for himself but he's sad for you. He wants you to let go of all the anger, and grief, and sadness. He wants you to live and be happy that you have found your True Self. He knows that your True Self, like his, knows that what happened is not real. That what *is* real is the eternal Mind and Spirit of your son. He is happy and free. He wants the same for you."

Completely deflated and torn between grief and rage, I slumped to the sand. Solomon sat down beside me and put his arm around me, keeping me upright. And again, I wept.

After what seemed like forever sitting on the beach, alternating between grief and hope, I was completely depleted, both physically and emotionally. The pull towards anger, grief, and depression was strong but eventually my faith in Solomon and God pulled me through. I refused to let the grief-induced depression take me and, on that little patch of beach, I fought for my soul. I had deluded myself for years about every conceivable subject. Now it was time to let my faith take over and save me from the world and myself. Sitting there on the beach, I felt Chris with me. I felt him stronger than I ever had before and I *knew* he was truly alive. That despite all appearances to the contrary, my son was alive and he was happy. His joy lifted me out of the darkness and saved me from the madness of hate, anger, and self-destruction.

"Chris saved my life today, Solomon," I finally spoke after several hours of silence. "He saved me when I could not save him. Isn't that ironic?"

"It's not irony, my son. It's the power of love. Let's get you back to the Inn so you can rest and heal."

And like a cripple leaning on his crutch, I leaned on this little old man as we walked back to my room. Despite my state, I couldn't help but marvel at how easily he bore my weight and kept me moving. I hit the bed sometime in the early afternoon and that was the last thing I remembered until the next morning.

The Whale

A light awaits me
At the end of yonder tunnel
A beacon of hope declining
The darkness that moves to surround me
Fueled by anger and shame
Trying to bar my way
Yet something much grander
Lives eternally within
Asking for leave to comfort
Waiting to embrace me again
For lost I have been
Reborn I must be
If ever my soul to survive
The evil that beckons me

A Day Off

As I awoke to the sounds of a new day beginning outside my window, I recalled my dreams of the night before. Dreams of floating free and dreams of lightness permeated my sleep and I felt like I could fly. But when I tried to fly away, I noticed a restraint around my ankle that kept me tethered to the ground. Despite the lightness of my body, although it really didn't feel like a body, I could not break free. I could feel the restriction but could not see what it was that continued to bind me. I continued to struggle, continued to try to fly until I awoke.

I endeavored to rise from my bed but didn't have the strength to do so. I wasn't even sure I could make it across the street today to see Solomon. As I was working on that dilemma, I heard a knock at my door. It was too early for Maria, my delightful room attendant. Still unable to motivate myself out of bed, I yelled out, "Who is it?"

"It's Solomon. You know, your friend from the beach," he replied, as I could envision him grinning from behind the door.

"Come in, it's not locked," I said, suddenly remembering I had indeed not locked the door. As he entered the room, clad in his usual attire of shorts, sandals, and Hawaiian shirt, I said, "You are truly a master of understatement, my old beach buddy."

"Well, you know my position on the use of words; as few as possible to make the point," he replied.

"Oh believe me, I know," I said, starting to feel a little better. "So Mohammed comes to the mountain, huh?"

"No lessons today, my friend. We are taking today off and I am escorting you to some of the most beautiful country you will ever see. I have a car and a driver and you and I can just sit back and enjoy."

So drive we did, and I saw some of the most beautiful coastline imaginable. We went to places I had never heard of, much less visited. And everywhere we went, Solomon had a story about someone there he knew and had helped. I imagine that he was probably a very big part of the beauty of those places. It seemed everywhere he went he elevated those around him. He was truly a very special man and he had spent much of his later years making a huge difference in people's lives. It was such a joy, riding and listening to his stories while winding along the exquisite coast. It was a virtual feast for the eyes, the ears, and the soul. And with every sight and story, I healed a little more, until by the end of our journey, my strength was back and I felt restored.

As we pulled into the Inn's parking lot, Solomon said to me, "Be well my friend. You have come far and tomorrow, we will have our final session. Tomorrow, you will be un-tethered. Now get out. The meter's running and this is really going to drive your bill up."

I leaned over and hugged him, and said, "Thank you Solomon. This meant a lot to me."

As I walked towards the entrance to the Inn, he said, "Sleep well and dream of *waking*."

Later, as I lay in my bed thinking about what Solomon had said, my mind went back to the night before and the dream of being tethered to the ground. It seemed odd that I had not even thought to mention it to him today. We had been together all day and we had not once mentioned dreams, or forgiveness, or any of the people in my life. I would ask him tomorrow during our last session. Our *last* session! It finally hit me that this would be our final time together. If tomorrow was to be our last session and my last lesson, what would it be? I had forgiven everyone I could think of and I had learned many wonderful things that would enrich my life forever. For the first time since Chris' death, I truly felt like I had let go of the murder and forgiven his killer. For the first time in a long while, hate, anger, and grief were not dictating my life. But there was still something deep inside that gnawed at me, something that was still not right. I felt better but not complete; something was missing. My last thought as the day's events finally overtook me and I drifted off into sleep, was that tomorrow would be the best lesson of all.

A Day Off

If beauty be in the eye of the beholder
Then where is evil born
Both are bred of mind we see
And so we must be torn
Between that which ails us
And raises our fists in rage
And the love that only comforts
And releases from worldly cage
So now I heal with love
From damage so painfully done
Beauty and peace my new companion
At long last I can see the Sun

The Last Lesson

The thought of this being possibly the last time I would see Solomon was a sobering way to wake up. Then the thought occurred to me that if this was the dream and spiritual oneness was the reality, then not only would this not be our final session, but I would be forever bonded to this diminutive but spiritual giant of a man. What had he said to me yesterday when we parted, *dream of waking*? If we got here by falling into a dream could we find our way out by awakening within the dream? Wasn't that what I was in the process of doing? Wasn't that what forgiveness was all about, letting go of the illusion until what was left was truth?

I had dreamed last night of being tethered again while attempting to fly. But this time, I looked down and Solomon was untying the rope that held me earthbound. He looked up at me and said, "*You were never truly bound. It was your belief that kept you in place and it was your unwillingness to be free that prevented your flight. Are you willing to be free Michael?*" His question and my hesitation to answer were the last things I remembered before waking.

Although the impending finality of the day inhibited me, the anticipation of what I would learn motivated me to shower, get dressed, and head for the café. As I dashed across the boulevard, I heard the loud screeching of brakes. I looked around to see one very upset motorist glaring at me as he leaned on his steering wheel. I stopped dead in my tracks and gestured a *sorry* and then got my butt out of the street.

"I didn't know you were *that* opposed to being free," Solomon said, with a grin and no trace of concern.

"Do you think I did that on purpose?" I replied, still shaken by the near squashing of my illusory body.

"Absolutely not, I *know* you did that on purpose. Just because you didn't do it consciously, doesn't mean you didn't do it intentionally," he replied, still grinning. "Buy me a cup of coffee and Danish and I'll tell you all about yourself."

"Damn it, Solomon. Doesn't anything ever rattle you?" I managed to eke out despite my clanging nerves.

"I don't get rattled over dreams, my young friend. I take them for what they are, information about our selves and directions to the exit."

"I should know better by now than to ask you a question that we both already know the answer to. I'll be back in a minute with the coffee."

Lisa greeted me with a rare smile as I approached the counter for my last cup of coffee at the café. Before I could return the favor, she placed two coffees and two chocolate Danish in front of me. "These are on the house, Monsieur. Any friend of Solomon is a friend to us. Solomon said you would be leaving soon. We will miss you. Please take care of yourself and come back to see us soon." Still dumbfounded by the graciousness of this small French lady who had just said more to me in the last few seconds than in the entire time I had been here, I said simply, "Thank you Lisa, I will."

As I carried the gifts to the table, Solomon looked up at me with what I swore was a tear in his eye. "It's about time. I thought you and Lisa were going to yap all day," he said, looking torn between affection and humor.

"*She* actually did most of the talking. But I think I just started believing in miracles. I could have sworn that woman couldn't stand me until a few seconds ago."

"Miracles have been happening all around you for a long time, my young schmoozer. You have been asleep but now you are starting to awaken."

We fell silent as Solomon turned his gaze to the sky and the ocean and I pondered what had just happened and been revealed. We ate and drank in complete silence until Solomon finally said, "Time for our last walk Michael, time to loosen the straps that bind you".

I looked at him with sadness in my heart, not wanting the time with this very unique and eloquent man to end. He had done so much for me. He had literally saved my life and soul. And now we would take our final walk on the beach and he would impart his wisdom to me one last time.

"Yes, Solomon," was all that was needed to say as we stood and walked towards the boundless ocean.

As we walked the seawall towards the beach, Solomon broke his usual silence and said, "Michael, this will be the happiest day of your life.

The Last Lesson

Sadness is for those who don't believe in eternal life. Our bodies may separate after today but our minds and souls never will. Know that I am, just like Chris, with you always," and then he stopped talking and continued walking.

This day, we walked along the beach in silence; watching the gliding pelicans, the surfer dolphins, and somewhere out of sight beneath the surface, my whale. After walking almost the length of the seawall on the beach, he stopped and looked directly into my eyes and spoke, "There is one last person to forgive, my dear friend. This will be your most rewarding lesson if you learn it."

"I'm not sure I want to hear what you have to say Solomon. Something in me fears this more than anything else you have told me, even though I don't know what it is."

"But you do know. That's *why* you fear it. Remember how you reacted when I told you that you hated your mother? Hate is born of both fear and guilt, which is what makes it so ominous and negative. But whether it's a parent or a murderer, it comes from the same place. When we all made the original mistake, or *sin* as the religions prefer to call it, we were immediately overcome with a sense of unimaginable regret. That regret over seemingly separating from our Creator was composed of guilt over having thrown away everything and fear of retaliation. In our oneness, we would have never conceived of either loss or retaliation but in separation we no longer had access to the truth. God did not evict us from the Garden of Eden. We chose to vacate and then punished ourselves with guilt, fear, and self-hate for having done so."

"So what does all that have to do with my fear?"

"It has everything to do with it. Above all else, your mother, your dad, and even your son's killer, you hate yourself the most. And your fear of confronting that is enormous. Your self-hate is your way of punishing yourself for not only leaving your Holy Father, but your son Chris as well. And you believe, in your separated mind, that you deserve every bit of it."

I stood there motionless and once again, stunned. After a few moments, I regained my composure. "I understand about leaving the garden, but what do you mean about leaving Chris? I never left Chris."

"I know you didn't, but you believe you did. According to your separated mind, you left him emotionally, you left him by working all the time, and you left him to die because you didn't protect him."

The Last Lesson

An instant war raged in my mind! Part of me wanted to strike back at this attack on my fatherhood and tell Solomon to *go to hell*. But the other part knew he was right and wanted to accept it and move on. After the battle raged within me for several minutes, my True Self spoke, "You are right my friend, I do believe all of those things," and I placed my hand on his shoulder in apology for my anger.

As I felt my body sag in resignation and acceptance of what I had done to my boy, I felt Solomon's arm around my shoulder as we both eased down to the sand. "Now that you've done the easy part, let's get to work," he said, with that same familiar smile on his face.

"If that's the easy part, I want my money back. This is too damn hard," I said, in a weak-hearted attempt at humor.

"There is one more thing you must do Michael to have your life back and your soul set on the right path. You must forgive yourself."

"But you were right Solomon, I did desert my son and it is the biggest regret of my life. There were so many times I should have been there. And all the time I spent trying to fix him should have been spent just loving and accepting him. I did work too much and I did separate from him emotionally. And I didn't protect him. And that was my worst failure, the one thing I swore I would always do for my children. Even if I wasn't worth a damn as a father, I could at least protect them, at least keep them out of harms way. I failed him in every way and I have no right to ask his forgiveness."

"You don't need Chris' forgiveness. He feels only love for you and holds no grievance whatsoever. He wants, more than anything, for you to forgive yourself. Not because you were a poor dad but because you never hurt him in any way. You all played a part in the drama of his life and death and you all consented to the script in order to learn and teach each other. Your lesson is, as is all of ours, *forgiveness*. Our Father has been trying to get us to forgive ourselves ever since we left the Garden because He, like Chris, knows that we never did anything wrong. We made a mistake and then we forgot to laugh at our folly. He wants us to be happy and know that He loves us and that there is absolutely nothing to forgive."

"I don't know if I can Solomon. I feel so guilty."

"For me, for your son, for yourself, and for your God; let it go my friend, just let it go."

And there on the sand in broad daylight, I both cried and laughed, and I let the guilt go. And for the first time in my life, I felt free. I knew beyond anything that anyone could ever say to me that I was free and no longer bound by anything except love. And a glorious and happy union it was! I felt connected to everything; to Solomon, to Chris, to the ocean and sky, and to every soul and thought ever created. And most of all, I knew my Father loved me and would for eternity. I was at peace, finally.

We sat on the beach in joyful silence knowing that words meant nothing and that we both shared everything worth having. We sat there until the sun went down over the horizon and then Solomon stood and said, "I will see you for one last cup of coffee tomorrow before you leave. Careful crossing the street and don't be late. Your family needs you." And he left.

The Last Lesson

Regret and remorse are but simple ways
To chain us to guilt's dark path
A way of keeping our soul repressed
Made victims of ego's wrath
To maintain us apart, the unholy goal
Forgive we must, to merge as one
Forgive ourselves, the only Son

Saying Goodbye

As I lay in bed feeling the best I had in a very long time, my mind turned to Solomon and all the amazing things he had taught me during these last astonishing days. This wonderful old man had not only changed my life, he had literally saved it. I felt true peace for perhaps the first time in my life and that hole in my soul that had been present for as long as I could remember, now seemed filled. I had renewed hope, happiness, and a knowing that everything true in the universe was as it should be. I also knew that my time here was over. It seemed odd to be both sad and happy at the same time but both were equally true. I had this overwhelming sense of completeness and I somehow knew that this wonderful gift I had been given was enough and that Solomon would move on, probably to help another lost soul. Today could be the last time I ever saw him but I was so grateful for what he had given me that even that could not dampen my joy.

I showered and dressed very slowly, wanting to savor every last moment. Finally, as I left the room and walked down the hallway of the Inn, I saw Maria. Maria, the lovely Latino woman who had cleaned my room during my stay smiled and said, "Hasta luego, Senor Miguel." How she knew I was leaving I had no idea but, after all that had happened, I didn't even question it. I stopped and said, "Thank you Maria. It's been a real pleasure knowing you," and I hugged her with a lack of restraint usually reserved for those closest to me. I finally released her and stood back. Maria had tears running down both cheeks and the gentlest of looks in her eyes. We simply nodded to each other, and I turned to leave. I considered stopping by the front desk but after Maria and the impending goodbye with Solomon, I didn't think I could handle any more emotion.

As I crossed the 101, I saw Solomon sitting in our usual place, smiling and talking to those around him. For the first time, I noticed how these people looked at him; a combination of awe, admiration, and genuine love. Obviously, he had affected a lot more people than me. "Hey old man,

Saying Goodbye

are you bothering the patrons again?" I said, unable to hide the affection I too felt for this man.

"You are finally happy, Michael. And you are ready to live your life," he said in his usual way of brushing aside the small talk and getting to the heart of the matter.

"Yes Solomon, I am," was all I said, and all I needed to say.

"Can I buy you one last cup of coffee?" he said.

"Absolutely." I replied, as he headed for the counter.

As we sat sipping our hot coffee on yet another *beautiful day in paradise*, I noticed how comforting the ocean breezes and sounds were and how they reminded me of an unseen peace I had found here.

"Solomon, you know there is absolutely no way that I could ever come close to repaying you for what you have done for me. And although money and gratitude are all I have to give, I know, or at least I think, you have to make a living too. So, mighty therapist from Heaven, how much do I owe you?"

He looked so far into my eyes that I swear he touched my soul and I felt truly loved, touched by something far exceeding anything the world had to offer. Finally, after what seemed like both forever and instantly, he replied, "Everything and nothing." And for once, I did not need my teacher to explain. I knew what he meant, so we just nodded and finished our coffee. I knew what he had given me could never be measured in monetary terms and that it was both invaluable and free.

"It's time for me to go, my dear friend," I spoke, as I rose from my chair, barely able to contain my feelings for this wonderful old man who had given me my life back.

"Yes," he said, as he stood and took my outstretched hand and just held it. We both stood there, me with tears now starting to come, and Solomon smiling as if joy was his alone. He reached up and took my head in his hands and pulled me gently towards him, and he kissed me on my forehead. "Goodbye, my brother. Live well and know that you are never alone."

We stood for one last moment, knowing that we were forever joined, bonded by a love that could only come from a divine source. I turned and headed for the Inn. After a few steps, I looked back and he was looking at me, smiling. We both nodded, and that was the last time I saw Solomon.

Saying Goodbye

I am as light as air
Heavy heart does not burden me
I carry my love to it
I raise my wings for it
My soul has been restored
I have been cleansed and made whole
I depart my friend, for now
Though never apart we be
Taking the love offered
Taking it home with me

Leaving Paradise

My heart was heavy and light, sad and happy. It was time to leave a place I had come to love and a man I had come to respect, admire, and cherish. I had learned more about myself and truth in the last few days than I had in my previous fifty two years. But I also missed my family and friends left behind. And as exquisite as California was, I missed Colorado. I missed hugging my girls and watching Grace handling them and our lives so artfully. And I missed my buddies and the cool crisp mountain air. And I couldn't wait to talk to Wayne, who started it all.

I booked a next day flight to Denver and I now had the rest of the day to think about things and time for one last drive down Highway 101. So I packed, grabbed a bite, and headed south towards San Diego. I had come to love this drive along the coast and the small coastal villages that lined it between Carlsbad and La Jolla. The drive was gorgeous as usual. The surf and the surfers with their long boards, the endless sand, all the smiling faces, and those wonderful breezes that feel like cool whispers from Heaven. As I drove down the coast with my windows down and a prevailing peace upon me, I thought of how much I would miss this place. But I had learned so much and my soul had been so exquisitely repaired that I wanted to get home and share my happiness with the people I loved. This little slice of Heaven I had been so privileged to experience would need to be left behind now so that I could live, truly live, the rest of my life. I had forgiven my son's killer and, more importantly, I had forgiven myself. I had reclaimed my life and I was determined to never let it slip away from me again.

So eventually the drive ended, the day was spent, and my stay was over. These were the last thoughts to run through my mind as I drifted off into sleep.

Leaving Paradise

Reborn, only to say goodbye
To beauty of earth and ocean
And magnificent days gone by
But now I see no loss
I hear no lonely cry
All that was gifted here
I see with joyful eye
Nothing to lose, nothing apart
Taking all of it with me
Leaving behind a piece of my heart

Homecoming

My flight was due to depart at 8:15am and I had to scramble to drop off the car and get to the airport in time. I had slept like a baby and got a late start. With my farewells spoken the day before, I just said a quick goodbye at the front desk and made a dash for the airport. I lucked out at the security line and before I knew it, I was sitting at the gate area with a good forty five minutes to spare. I was going home.

The flight back gave me time to think about things but my mind was at peace and silent. I used to be the kind of guy whose mind raced along at a million miles an hour, always trying to anticipate, plan, and stay a couple of moves ahead of everyone else. That compulsion was now gone. I felt whole and I felt peaceful. For maybe the first time in my life, I didn't feel like I had anything to prove to anyone. So I just relaxed, and before I knew it, I had done something I had never done before, slept on an airplane.

I awoke to a gentle nudge by the stewardess asking me to *fasten my seat belt in preparation for landing.* How many times I had heard that statement before, but now even those overused, mundane words seemed different. I was coming to the conclusion that I was seeing the world through completely different eyes, eyes that I never knew I had. As the plane touched down at DIA, I felt that old familiar feeling of home. It was nice to be back but I knew that it would never be the same and that realization made me very happy. Despite all the career success, material wealth, and status I had managed to achieve in my life, I now knew that I had something none of that could buy. I had found peace and a joy in the simple act of living. I had found my center, my lost soul, and a union with my Creator that I never knew was possible. And all of it because of a few walks along the beach with a gentle, white haired, old man with the wisdom of Solomon.

I was a bit disappointed when I walked into the gate waiting area and saw no one to greet me. But that dissatisfaction almost immediately turned into contentment born of the certainty of being truly loved, loved

Homecoming

not just by Grace and the girls, but loved by a power I couldn't even see; loved by my God in a way that I would never again doubt.

I hailed a cab outside the terminal and I was on my way home at last. I hadn't given Grace much notice but she knew when I would be there. As we pulled onto my street, I was struck by how many cars were parked on the curb. Somebody having a party, I guess. I never even asked how much the fare was as I handed the cabbie a $100 bill. I could tell I had made his day and, as he looked at me in appreciation, I couldn't help but say "God loves you my friend," as I turned and walked up the driveway to my front door.

As I opened the door, I could hear voices in the backyard and saw my old buddy Tom grabbing a handful of beers and head out the back door. I set my luggage down, grabbed one out of the fridge for myself, and opened the door. There, in my backyard, among the mixing of voices and the smell of steaks on the grille, was my wife, my daughters, and virtually every friend I had in Colorado.

"I see my lovely wife has been whooping it up since I've been gone. By the way, who invited all you people anyway?"

The almost instant response of that many people saying my name in unison gave me chills. And as I stood there soaking it all in, I knew that everyone of us is connected in a way that exceeds our understanding. The moment was interrupted by the three women in my life all throwing their arms around me at once. The words, "Dad, we missed you so much" and "I sure missed my man" were like celestial music to my ears.

After all the kissing and hugging and hand shaking subsided, I sat down and dried my eyes. How could I have spent so much of my life not knowing how loved I was? It was always there and I never saw it. As I sat there, overwhelmed by all of the attention, it came to me that I had seen everyone except Wayne.

Almost immediately, I heard the words "Looking for me, old friend?" come from behind me. For an instant, I could have sworn that it was Solomon's voice. But as I turned, I saw Wayne standing there.

"Yes, indeed, I was looking for you. I've got a bone to pick with you, good buddy. Let's take a walk."

We went through the house and walked the neighborhood. I waved to a few of the neighbors but we kept moving. After a period of walking in silence, Wayne finally turned to me and said, "So how did you like Solomon?" I felt a huge smile come over me as I started to answer and

Homecoming

Wayne started laughing. "No need to answer. I can see it in your face," he added, between the chuckles.

"He changed my life, Wayne. That little old man literally saved my mortal life and my immortal soul. I'm not sure I would even be standing here talking to you if I hadn't met him. I really must thank you for sending me to him and for *not* being my therapist," I said, with a wry grin I had recently learned somewhere.

He laughed again and said, "That's okay, I figured you for a lost cause anyway. You've always been a bit too materialistic for my tastes."

"You better laugh when you say that you old hippie," I replied. It sure was good to see him again.

Eventually, we returned to the party and I spent the rest of the afternoon reveling in the warmth of being surrounded by so many good people, all of whom seemed genuinely pleased to see me again. Later, people started trickling out and eventually the crowd dwindled down to just my family and Wayne. I walked Wayne to the door and hugged him before he left. "You're a good friend," I said, as he headed for that old blue pickup of his. He looked back and just nodded.

The girls kissed me on both cheeks at the same time and headed for Amy's car. "We love you dad," I heard them say in unison, as they pulled out. Grace gently took my hand as we stood there on the front porch watching our beautiful daughters drive away. "We thought we might have lost you for awhile there," she whispered in my ear.

"I know. I lost me for awhile. But I'm back now and I know what a treasure I have. And I will never let anything take me away again. I've learned forgiveness Gracie, and it has made me a new man. I will never value the things that don't matter again and I will never forget to value the things that do. And I know now that you and the girls are blessings from God and I will always treasure you."

We both just stood there quietly holding each other. After a couple of the neighbors walked by and smiled that *get a room* look at us, we thought it might be time to take it inside. We both laughed and as Grace headed towards the door, I stopped her. "My love, I know I just got home but I need to take some time and absorb all of this. You sit down and relax and I'll be back in a little while and help you clean up." Without a word, she smiled, nodded, and went inside. I got in my car and headed for my favorite spot to think.

Homecoming

I see so clearly now
As doom has left my door
The gifts of love delivered
Mine forever more

A New Beginning

As Michael sat on the park bench gazing across the small lake at the snow-capped Rockies, he thought about how far he had come and everything that had happened to get him to this point. His only son had died a violent death, he had come close to a suicidal demise himself, and he had almost lost his family and his career. On the other hand; he had healed, he rediscovered a lost friendship, and he remembered an ancient one, *with me*. I will forever be a part of Michael's mind and heart, for we have become one in our Father. My heart overflows with love as I hear those same sweet words go through his mind and know that he will be safe and whole now. My work is done.

Amazing grace, how sweet the sound
that saved a wretch like me!
I once was lost, but now am found,
was blind, but now I see.

www.ingramcontent.com/pod-product-compliance
Lightning Source LLC
Chambersburg PA
CBHW070248100426
42743CB00011B/2187